DAMAGED BY GOD

A CRITICAL ANALYSIS OF 'COVERING THEOLOGY' WITH PARTICULAR REFERENCE TO JOHN BEVERE'S *UNDER COVER*

By

Allan Thomas Clare

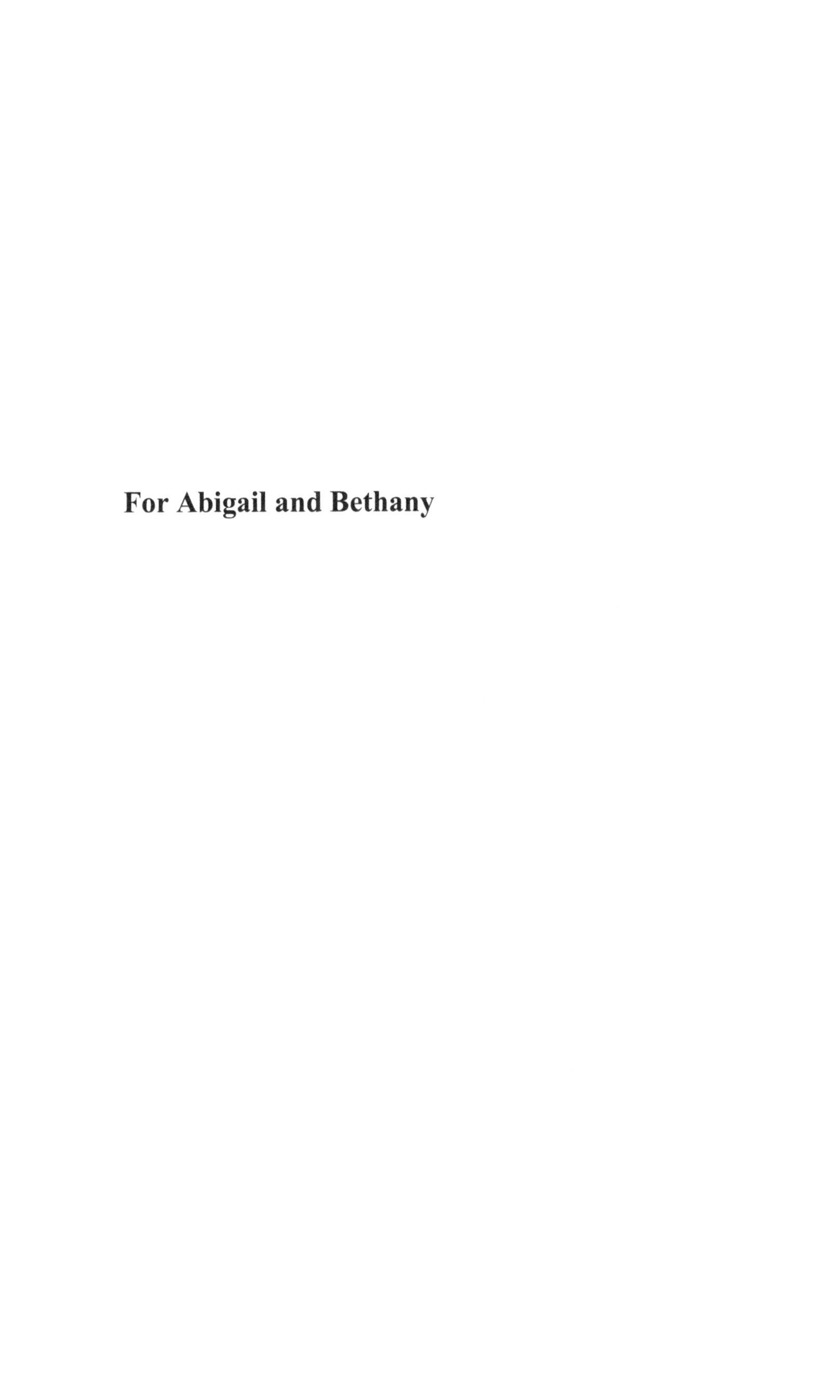

For Abigail and Bethany

Foreword

As I write, the UK is still under lockdown as a result of the Covid-19 pandemic. The decision to go into lockdown and the many debates about the nature of the Lockdown have led to a wider questioning of what it means to be under authority and what it means to obey rules laid down by other people.

Christians of varying denominations and traditions have struggled with how to understand the nature of authority and the issue goes to the heart of the Christian life. All of us recognise the need to accept advice and counsel about our life with Christ, but there is a great diversity of opinion about what that might look like! The Roman Catholic Church has always had a structured model of authority which, although it has often failed horrifically – one thinks of the abuse scandals of recent decades – has also been, when it works well, a strong model of how individuals can grow in Christian community. In Protestantism there has been a strong reaction against a Catholic and hierarchical model of Church, however, the biblical 'priesthood of all believers' model has often been usurped by too close a reliance on the authority and the charisma of the Pastor.

In Allan Clare's fascinating study (originally a thesis submitted for a Master of Arts (Contemporary Church Leadership) at the University of Wales (Trinity St. David) in 2012) he explores the contours of one particular model of authority which became known as the Shepherding Movement. In some ways this is a sad story of

Christians who wanted with great earnestness to take the call to discipleship seriously and were willing to recognise that they as individuals didn't have all the answers and needed to seek help, support and even a willingness to be obedient to other individuals who they felt were further along the path than they were.

I knew nothing of the Shepherding Movement before reading this book, but the book provides a wonderful and insightful study into our common human desire to seek community, love and acceptance beyond the confines of the individual. It allows us to see the pitfalls of making ourselves subject to other's authority in a way which lacks clear boundaries.

At its best the Church community can still offer a beautiful model of shared love and acceptance of difference. All of us are still seeking to discern what this might look like. We cannot always get it right and we make many mistakes along the way. To be faithful members of a Christian community is surely to recognise our faults, to seek forgiveness and to know God's love for us wherever we are on the journey. May we find wise and holy guides along the way.

Yours in Christ,

Fr. Phil Ritchie

Vicar of St Mary and St John Church, Oxford.

23rd June 2020

'…the Son of man came not to be served but to serve, and to give his life a ransom for many.'

Matthew 20:28

TABLE OF CONTENTS

CHAPTER ONE

A LITTLE HISTORY: THE SHEPHERDING MOVEMENT

"What experience and history teach us is that people and governments have never learned anything from history, or acted on principles deduced from it."

Georg Wilhelm Friedrich Hegel (1770 - 1831).

According to the *New International Dictionary of Pentecostal and Charismatic Movements* the Shepherding Movement (sometimes known as the Discipling Movement) emerged as a 'distinct nondenominational movement' in 1974.[1] In 1970 a group of four Charismatic Bible teachers met together in response to a ministerial impropriety at the Holy Spirit Teaching Mission (HSTM).[2] The four were Bernard (Bob) Mumford, ordained through the Assemblies of God; Derek Prince, another Pentecostal; Don Basham, an ordained Disciples of Christ minister; and Charles Simpson, originally a Southern Baptist. The men were already frequent contributors to

---

[1] Stanley M. Burgess and Eduard M. Van Der Maas, "The Shepherding Movement," *TNIDPCM*, 1060.

[2] The Holy Spirit Teaching Mission was a charismatic ministry in Fort Lauderdale, Florida, and had seen its founder, Eldon Purvis, resign. Purvis went on to found 'New Beginnings' which amalgamated aspects of Pentecostalism and British-Israel Covenant-keeping teachings. He died in 1990. Even now, the exact reason behind his resignation from HSTM is unclear.

New Wine magazine, published by the HSTM, and soon to become the biggest selling Charismatic periodical in the United States.[3] The four decided to mutually submit to one another and to hold each other accountable, and it was through *New Wine* that the peculiar teachings of the Shepherding Movement were emphasised and promoted: authority, submission, discipleship, commitment in covenant relationships, loyalty, pastoral care, and spiritual covering. S. David Moore, in his definitive account of the movement, summarises the key distinctive as:

> *...the need for discipleship through personal pastoral care or, as they termed it, 'shepherding' care... a believer was to submit to a 'personal pastor' who would help the individual develop Christian maturity.[4]*

Much has been said in analysis of why the Shepherding Movement emerged. William Kay says it can be seen as a 'response to growing individualism and the directionless flow of the Charismatic movement.'[5] By June 1974, when a second 'Shepherds Conference' in New Columbia attracted nearly 2,000 pastors and

---

[3] At its peak *New Wine* had over 90,000 subscriptions, a much larger figure at that time than *Christianity Today*. Although New Wine retained its title, in May 1972 HSTM changed its name to Christian Growth Ministries (CGM).

[4] S. David Moore, The Shepherding Movement: Controversy and Charismatic Ecclesiology (London: T & T Clark International, 2003), 1-2. Moore writes that 'the movement's teachings are complex and are a worthy topic for future study. The five leaders developed a complicated, dynamic, and nuanced theological and ecclesiological stance uncharacteristic of the theologically shallow stereotype often ascribed to Pentecostals and Charismatics' (p. 68).

[5] William K. Kay, *Apostolic Networks in Britain: New Ways of Being Church* (Milton Keynes: Paternoster Press, 2007), 195.

leaders, the four had become five with the addition to the group of Canadian Pentecostal W.J.E. (Ern) Baxter. Together they became known as the 'Fort Lauderdale Five'. One year later, in Kansas City, the 1975 National Men's Shepherds Conference was attended by nearly 5,000 Charismatic leaders and there was a growing stream of churches submitting to the 'Five'. The number of adherents directly involved was estimated at over 100,000. *New Wine* magazine and the use of new media (video and audio cassette tapes) promulgating the Shepherding emphases were shipped across the United States and the world. Moore says that statistics for the five-year period from 1979 - 1984 show a distribution of four and a half million magazines, one million newsletters, six hundred thousand cassette tapes and a quarter of a million books.[6]

The rise in influence alarmed many, who saw in the Shepherding Movement, despite the protestations and denials of the five men, a new Charismatic denomination forming.[7] Added to this were tales of abusive authority, hyper-submission and controlled lives. In 1975 Pat Robertson, founder of the Christian Broadcasting Network (CBN), denounced the movement for 'cultic' excesses and banned any CBN-affiliated media from working with the Five. Robertson wrote an open letter to Bob Mumford with many

---

[6] Moore, *Shepherding*, 7.

[7] Steven Lambert sarcastically contends that 'this elite ministerial Quintumverate' concluded that the burgeoning charismatic movement needed 'some good, old-fashioned human organisation, man-centered authoritarianism, and ecclesiastical hierarchy.' Steven Lambert, *Charismatic Captivation: Authoritarian Abuse and Psychological Enslavement in Neo-Pentecostal Churches* (Chapel Hill NC: Real Truth Publications, 2003), 3,24.

allegations from former Shepherding members of abusive spiritual authority. In the same year Demos Shakarian, founder of the Full Gospel Businessmen's Fellowship International (FGBMFI), forbade any chapter of the FGBMFI to promote the shepherding teachings, while Charismatic healing evangelist Kathryn Kuhlman refused to share a platform at the Jerusalem Holy Spirit Conference with Bob Mumford. The latter withdrew.

In an effort to deal with the controversy, Charismatic leaders met with the five Shepherding leaders at the Curtis Hotel, Minneapolis. The meeting has entered Charismatic folklore as 'the shoot-out at the Curtis Hotel,' an epitaph which indicates the prevailing atmosphere.[8] Separate tracks followed for the 1977 Kansas City Conference on Charismatic Renewal and, despite the controversies, more than 9,000 attended the Shepherding track, with only 1,500 attending the non-Shepherding sub-conference.[9]

Accusations of spiritual abuse continued. In 1976, the 'Five' issued a statement of concern and regret:

We realise that controversies and problems have arisen among Christians in various areas as a result of our teaching in relation to subjects such as submission, authority, discipling, shepherding. We deeply regret these problems

---

[8] For the definitive account of this, and the Shepherding Movement in its entirety, see Moore, *Shepherding*.

[9] The Shepherding track came second to the Catholic Charismatics with 25,000 attendees.

and, insofar as they are due to fault on our part, we ask forgiveness from our fellow believers whom we have offended.[10]

By 1980 it was clear that many members and churches were haemorrhaging from the movement. Derek Prince publicly exited in 1984, (having privately severed his ties with the group in 1983), citing a change of theological direction: he no longer believed in trans-local pastoral submission and said that the group had been 'guilty of the Galatian error: having begun in the Spirit, we quickly degenerated into the flesh.'[11] In 1986 *New Wine* ceased publication and the remaining four men ended their formal relationship. The Shepherding Movement seemed to be over.

Don Basham died in 1989.[12] In November of that year Bob Mumford read a statement at the Christian Believers United meeting in North Carolina. The statement made the cover of *Ministries Today* magazine in the January / February edition of 1990 which simply read: 'Discipleship was wrong. I repent. I was wrong. I ask for forgiveness. - Bob Mumford.'[13] Mumford publicly repented of his part in the Shepherding Movement, admitting 'some families were split up and lives turned upside down. Some of these families are

---

[10] Cited in Moore, *Shepherding*, 102.

[11] Prince went on to say, 'I repented of my involvement and renounced the error. I deeply regret the damage that was done to the body of Christ and in the lives of many promising young men and women.'

[12] Ern Baxter died in July 1993 and Derek Prince in September 2003.

[13] Jamie Buckingham, "The End of the Discipleship Era," *MT* (January/February 1990): 46.

still not back together.' There was an admittance that the movement had caused 'an unhealthy submission resulting in perverse and unbiblical obedience to human leaders.'[14]

Moore's exhaustive account of the movement concludes that the very things that the Shepherding Movement taught:

> *...created a propensity toward an abuse of spiritual authority, especially among young immature leaders, or leaders who lacked character and integrity...the emphasis on hierarchically oriented submission to God's delegated authorities led to many cases of improper control and abusive authority throughout the movement.*[15]

---

[14] Buckingham, "Discipleship," 48.

[15] Moore, *Shepherding*, 149, 182.

CHAPTER TWO

FROM SHEPHERDING TO UNDER COVER

The September 1972 issue of *New Wine* had presented the first of a series of seven articles by Bob Mumford which 'focused on the need for practical obedience to God and submission to his delegated authority in all spheres of life.'[16] In October 1972 Charles Simpson's article on the 'Covering of the Lord' appeared. In this, Simpson focused on the 'covering' or protection provided by submitting oneself to God's delegated authority in the home, church, and civil government.'[17] Despite the near-history of the Shepherding Movement, and despite it being a mere eleven years since Mumford's very public apology, in 2001 Thomas Nelson published John Bevere's *Under Cover*, a book which promotes Bevere's own teachings on authority, submission, discipleship, commitment in covenant relationships, loyalty, pastoral care, and spiritual covering.

Bevere's book has been a best-seller. It has been translated into over twenty languages and is often found in the bookshops of Charismatic churches, perhaps more so, as one reviewer says, in those churches that are 'accustomed to top-down, hierarchical models of church leadership.'[18] Leighton Tebay contends that 'while

---

[16] Moore, *Shepherding*, 54.

[17] Moore, Shepherding, 55. In 2012, the magazine was obtainable at www.csmpublishing.org/pdf/newwine/101972.pdf

[18] Tyler Ramey, "What's Wrong with John Bevere's *Under Cover?*" n.p. [cited 21 November 2011]. Online: http://www.truth-enterprises.com/ (Obtainable in 2012).

covering theology is more popular in non-denominational Charismatic churches it is slowly gaining ground in more traditional Evangelical circles.'[19]

As there is only one appearance of the word 'covering' in the entire New Testament - used in connection with a woman's head covering in 1 Cor 11:15 - some have argued there is 'scant biblical evidence to support it.'[20] However, the absence of the word 'Trinity' in the Bible does not equate to scanty biblical evidence for this truth. The question should not be, 'Is this particular word in the Bible?' but instead 'Is this is a biblical principle?' Steven Lambert writes that, because of the rejection of Shepherding teaching in the 1970s and 1980s, proponents of the doctrine began to implement 'alternate, less overt terminology.[21] Mary Alice Chrnalogar agrees:

> *...since many leaders in the Shepherding Movement admitted doing wrong, various people who continue to use the same methods have begun to give different labels for the same actions... The errors are covered in many different terms like delegated authority, covering, unquestioned submission, covenant, commitment to a fellowship, etc. Terms change from time to time. Submission may be called 'commitment,'*

---

[19] Leighton Tebay, "Covering and Authority," n.p. [cited 21 November 2011]. Online: http://coveringandauthority.com/ The term 'covering theology' will be used for the teaching in *Under Cover*. (Obtainable in 2012).

[20] Frank Viola, *Reimagining Church: Pursuing the Dream of Organic Christianity* (Colorado Springs: David C. Cook, 2008), 203.

[21] Lambert, *Captivation*, 79.

'covenant relationship' or 'divine order' in church government. Many times terms aren't used at all; it is the actions that tell you what is going on.[22]

It has been said that the original teachers in the Discipleship / Shepherding Movement 'established a beachhead from which others have advanced.[23] Although Bevere avoids using the words 'shepherding' and 'discipleship' throughout *Under Cover*, the main focus of the book is teaching on obedience to 'delegated authority' and the 'spiritual covering' it provides. But does the New Testament teach that we are protected from spiritual attack or error through submission to a church leader? What is entailed by 'spiritual covering' and who exactly is God's 'delegated authority' in the Church? And how much authority is delegated to him or her?

---

[22] Mary Alice Chrnalogar, *Twisted Scriptures: Breaking Free From Churches That Abuse* (Grand Rapids: Zondervan, 1997), 23.

[23] Moore, *Shepherding*, 191.

CHAPTER THREE
DELEGATED AUTHORITY

Covering theology is inextricably linked with the concept of 'delegated authority' which comes from Romans 13. Bevere's first reference to this scripture occurs on page 11 after the following comment:

> *Some may say, 'I submit to God, but not to man, unless I agree with him.' This is where our upbringing and incorrect church thinking can hinder us. We cannot separate our submission to God's inherent authority from our submission to His delegated authority. All authority originates from Him!*[24]

The first two verses of Romans chapter 13 are then cited, with the words 'For there is no authority except from God,' italicized (in bold typeface here):

> *Let every soul be subject to the governing authorities. **For there is no authority except from God**, and the authorities that exist are appointed by God. Therefore whoever resists the authority resists the ordinance of God, and those who resist will bring judgment on themselves (Rom 13:1-2).*

Bevere points out that the words 'Let every soul' mean that

---

[24] Ibid., 11.

'no one is exempt...It is a command, not a suggestion,' before correctly teaching that the Greek word for 'subject' in the passage is ὑποτάσσω, which, according to Thayer's Greek dictionary is, in non-military usage, 'a voluntary attitude of giving in, cooperating, assuming responsibility, and carrying a burden.' He summarises the meaning of ὑποτάσσω as a word that 'exhorts us to voluntarily place ourselves under submission to authorities with the full intent of obeying them,'[25] and identifies that the English word 'appointed' in these verses is the Greek word τάσσω: '...which means 'to assign, ordain, or set.' In no way does this word have 'by chance' implications. It is direct appointment.[26]

Bevere then uses some scriptural examples (such as the story of Joseph) which show the sovereignty of God in the setting up of various 'authorities' in the Bible. In all this, Bevere is teaching what Ron Burks called 'the Shepherding Movement's now infamous doctrine.'[27] Derek Prince, in the Shepherding Movement's key text *Shepherding, Discipleship, Commitment*, wrote:

> *...the New Testament requires submission to the following specific relationships...all Christians to secular government on all levels...all Christians to those who rule over them in the church...we do not obey those in authority because they*

---

[25] Ibid., 88.

[26] Ibid., 88.

[27] Ron & Vicki Burks, *Damaged Disciples: Casualties of Authoritarian Churches and the Shepherding Movement* (Grand Rapids: Zondervan, 1992), 136.

are right; we obey them because they are in authority, and all authority ultimately stems from God himself (See Rom 13:1-5)... Our attitude toward those who whom God sets in delegated authority over us is the outward and visible expression of our attitude toward God himself.[28]

Such linking of delegated authority to church leaders, and therefore church leaders to God's authority, is also seen in Watchman Nee's *Spiritual Authority*, a book often cited by the Shepherding Movement and by Bevere.[29] Nee writes:

God is the source of all authorities in the universe... Wherever people encounter authority they meet God...Is there any room for us to choose between God's direct authority and his delegated authority? No, we must be subject to delegated authority as well as to God's direct authority, for 'there is no authority except from God.'[30]

Applying Romans 13 not only to civil authorities but to church leaders is the major building block in covering theology. Bevere writes, with no explanation, that 'these words of exhortation

---

[28] Derek Prince, *Discipleship, Shepherding, Commitment* (Ft Lauderdale: Derek Prince Publications, 1976), 19.

[29] On the back of the May 1972 *New Wine*, Bob Mumford recommends Nee's '*Spiritual Authority*' and says, 'Spiritual authority... is what the Master is saying to his Body of Christ across this nation.' Bob Mumford, "A Most Timely Book," *NW* (May 1972). The magazine, along with every edition of *New Wine* from June 1969 to December 1983, can be accessed at http://www.csmpublishing.org (Obtainable in 2012).

[30] Watchman Nee, *Spiritual Authority* (New York: Christian Fellowship Publishers, 1972), 61.

apply not only to governmental leaders but also encompass other areas of delegated authority. What we glean from this text should be applied to all areas of delegated authority.'[31] These areas of delegated authority are 'civil, church, family, and social.'[32] Bevere reiterates that disobeying these delegated authorities is the same as disobeying God:

> *Since God has appointed all authorities, we refuse the authority behind them if we dishonour or refuse to submit to them. Whether we know it or not, we resist the ordinance or rule of God. When we oppose God's delegated authority, we oppose God Himself!*[33]

The results of disobedience are severe:

> *...most Christians think obedience is the exception and personal free choice is the rule. Following this type of reasoning can lead us into a course of destruction. The consequences...are severe. Not only does it place us under the judgment of God, but it grants legal access to demonic powers. If we want to remain obedient to God and we have but one choice when it comes to delegated authority - submission and obedience.*[34]

---

[31] Bevere, *Under*, 87.

[32] Ibid., 88.

[33] Ibid., 88.

[34] Ibid., 89.

The key question is: does Romans 13:1-6 refer to anything other than civil authorities? Covering theology contends that everyone should submit to those in authority over them (whether a husband, church leader or employer) and that everyone who is in authority (and their authority is inherent in their position) is God's delegated authority. Therefore, those who resist God's delegated authority are resisting God.

One must first read the whole passage to see the context of these opening verses. These passages are clearly referring to state authorities, civil governments and officials, and cannot be used to refer to God's delegated authorities in the family or church. The first six verses of Romans chapter 13 are the context, and there are three obvious applications to the state authorities that simply cannot be attributed to church authorities. The first is seen in verse four: 'For he is God's servant to do you good. But if you do wrong, be afraid, for he does not bear the sword for nothing' (Rom 13:4). This bearing of the sword is often used to claim God's approval of capital punishment - an argument beyond the scope of this essay - but the obvious point is that bearing a sword of punishment is not a role for authorities within the Church. The second application to civil authorities is seen in their retributive function on wrongdoers:

He is God's servant, an agent of wrath to bring punishment on the wrongdoer. Therefore, it is necessary to submit to the authorities, not only because of possible punishment but also because of conscience (Rom 13:4-5).

Again, wrath on wrongdoers is not a function of the New Testament church. And thirdly, and perhaps most clearly, the authorities that Paul is describing in these verses are linked to taxation:

> *This is also why you pay taxes, for the authorities are God's servants, who give their full time to governing. Give everyone what you owe him: If you owe taxes, pay taxes; if revenue, then revenue; if respect, then respect; if honour, then honour (Rom 13:6-7).*

There is no doubt that the New Testament urges the believer to obey civil authorities. Paul writes to Timothy:

> *I urge, then, first of all, that requests, prayers, intercession and thanksgiving be made for everyone - for kings and all those in authority, that we may live peaceful and quiet lives in all godliness and holiness (1 Tim 2:1-2).*

Titus is instructed to 'remind the people to be subject to rulers and authorities, to be obedient, to be ready to do whatever is good' (Titus 3:1). Peter writes to the believers to 'submit yourselves for the Lord's sake to every authority instituted among men: whether to the king, as the supreme authority, or to governors, who are sent by him to punish those who do wrong and to commend those who do right...fear God, honour the King' (1 Pet 2:13-14,17). And Christ himself taught his followers to 'Give to Caesar what is Caesar's and to God what is God's...' (Mark 12:17).

There is no scriptural warrant, however, to insist that what is gleaned from these verses in Romans 'should be applied to all areas of delegated authority.'[35] The context and examples are clearly related to civil government. Mark Vrankovich writes:

Those trying to twist scripture often take verses out of context by viewing the verse in isolation to the verses around it. However, here we have an instance of verses being taken out of context when the context is contained within the quoted verses.[36]

The New Testament is devoid of church leaders who 'bear the sword,' are 'agents of wrath to bring punishment on the wrong doer,' or who collect taxes and revenue. One commentator has also pointed out that 'in the shift to spiritual authority' that Bevere's interpretation envisions, the judgment mentioned in the passage is turned into 'a direct spiritual judgment from God - something nowhere even suggested in the passage.'[37]

Such a view of Romans 13, leads to statements such as the following. Terry Nance, another advocate of covering theology, says:

---

[35] Ibid., 87.

[36] Mark Vrankovich, "Church Leadership Authority," n.p. [cited 21 November 2011]. Online: http://www.cultwatch.com/ChurchLeadershipAuthority.html (Obtainable in 2012).

[37] M. James Sawyer, "Under Cover: Authority, Obedience (& Abuse?)" n.p. [cited 21 November 2011]. In 2012, obtainable online at: http://www.reclaimingthemind.org/blog/2009/04/under-cover-authority-obedience-abuse/

...you must have it settled in your heart that according to Romans 13:1-2, all authority is ordained of God. You must make up your mind to submit to your pastor in the same way that you would submit to Jesus...to refuse to submit to God's delegated authority is to refuse to submit to God.[38]

Paul does indeed use the verb ὑποτάσσω meaning 'to subject, to subordinate,'[39] but the noun to which submission is required – ἐξουσίαις - ('authorities') is never used of leaders in the church.[40] It is, as Moo says, 'a phrase that is central to the interpretation of the passage,'[41] but there is no scholarly debate over whether this passage in Romans 13 refers to church leaders as well as civil authorities. The debate in the text, again beyond the scope of this essay, is a debate about whether Christians should voluntarily submit and be

---

[38] Terry Nance, *God's Armor Bearer: Serving God's Leaders* (Shippensburg: Destiny Image Publishers, 2003), 19.

[39] BDAG, s.v. ὑποτάσσω 1a. Some translations use the English word 'obey' but the New Testament expresses this through ὑπακούω, πειθαρχέω, or πείθομαι.

[40] Instead, in its plural form, Paul's use of ἐξουσίαις, consistently refers to 'spirit authorities' as in Eph 3:10; 6:12 and Col 1:13,16. However, such consistency in translating the word as 'spiritual authorities' is supported in every case by the context in which the word appears - *except* here in Romans 13. Additionally, when ἐξουσίαι is referring to spiritual beings, Paul always uses ἀρχαί as well – this is missing in Rom 13:1. Josephus also uses the plural of the word to refer to the Roman authorities in Judea (Bell. ii.350).

[41] Douglas J. Moo, The Epistle to the Romans (NICNT; Grand Rapids: Eerdmans, 1996), 795.

obedient to a corrupt government.[42] Douglas Moo writes that 'it is only a slight exaggeration to say that the history of the interpretation of Romans 13:1-7 is the history of attempts to avoid what seems to be its plain meaning,'[43] while another has said of the passage, 'these seven verses have caused more unhappiness and misery in the Christian East and West than any other seven verses in the New Testament.'[44] But the debate over what is the 'plain meaning' of the text (which can be summarised in the question 'Are Christians required to obey the government's orders at all times and in every situation?') is not a debate over whether Paul had the authority of church leaders in mind. Modern scholarly commentaries do not even broach this subject when looking at the text, and it is only in looking at writers who advocate 'covering theology' and 'delegated

---

[42] Leighton Tebay, in seeking to show that there is leeway in these verses to resist corrupt and harsh government, has written: 'Paul has chosen to be very precise in his wording in Romans 13. If he meant to say people are resisting God if they resist authority he would have said that. Instead, he said that those who resist authority are resisting what God ordained or put in order.' He then uses the example of a parking lot manager, who is appointed to be an authority in the parking lot, but who then commands a worker to break company policy: 'A worker may end up in total rebellion against the manager but still completely respect and follow the wishes of the ultimate authority.' Tebay, "Covering," n.p. Additionally, Mary Alice Chrnalogar writes 'notice the words 'for rulers hold no terror for those who do right' This passage only refers to good government, because those who do right under good government have no fear of the rulers. Under corrupt leaders, there is fear of doing what truly is right.' Chrnalogar, *Twisted*, 90

[43] Moo, *Romans*, 806.

[44] Cited by Leon Morris, *The Epistle to the Romans* (Grand Rapids: Eerdmans, 1988), 457.

authority' can you find any such debate.[45]

---

[45] Fitzmyer points out that even in medieval and Renaissance times, when the Church and the State were often one and the same, commentators were 'divided over whether Paul was referring solely to civil rulers.' Cajetan, Seripando, Melanchthon, and Calvin interpreted the passage as referring to civil rulers, whereas Sadoleto and Luther understood it as 'spiritual rulers' and 'secular princes'. But, as Fitzmyer concludes, 'This distinction rarely surfaces in the modern discussion of the text' Joseph A. Fitzmyer, *Romans* (AYBC 33; New York: Doubleday, 1993), 666.

CHAPTER FOUR

'THE KINGDOM OF GOD' IN BEVERE'S THOUGHT: RANK, ORDER AND AUTHORITY

One reason that Bevere sees Romans 13 as applicable to church authorities is his view of the kingdom of God. The jump from Paul's command to be subject to governmental authorities to the supposed command of being subject to *church* authorities can be linked to Bevere's view of God's kingdom as described in Chapter 2 of *Under Cover*. He writes:

> *My experience has been that Westerners (dwellers of democratic nations of America and Europe) are some of the most resistant people to truly hearing the word of God. The reason is fundamental. It is hard to understand kingdom principles with a democratic mind-set. Democracy is fine for the nations of the world, but we must remember the kingdom of God is just that - a kingdom. It is ruled by a King, and there are rank, order, and authority.*[46]

Bevere follows up this assertion with a reminder of the potentially dire consequences for those who do not agree:

> *If we attempt to live as believers with a cultural mind-set towards authority, we will be at best ineffective and at worst*

---

[46] Bevere, *Under*, 10.

positioned for danger. Our provision as well as protection could be blocked or even cut off as we disconnect ourselves from the Source of true life.[47]

Bevere is treading old Shepherding ground. In 1976, responding to what they termed the 'Discipleship and Submission Movement,' the General Council of the Assemblies of God wrote:

...some of these teachers claim their mission and the church's mission is no longer evangelism, but the setting up of a new order on earth in prospect of bringing in the Kingdom. But the New Testament does not indicate we can set up a purified external order in this age. The Church grows and develops, but the tares will be among the wheat until the harvest. Judgement that destroys the present world order is necessary before the kingdom rule can be established on earth, as Daniel 2, 2 Thessalonians 1, and Revelation 19 clearly indicate.[48]

The fact that God's kingdom is a spiritual reality is not alluded to by Bevere. As such, with the Church as 'the kingdom here and now', a hierarchical model of rank and authority is set up. This is the same ecclesiology that Moore evaluates in his account of the Shepherding Movement. He writes:

---

[47] Ibid., 10.

[48] The full paper of this session can be found online at http://www. ministers.ag.org/pdf/Discipleship.pd [cited 21 November, 2011] (Obtainable in 2012).

The movement's ecclesiology was founded upon its view of the kingdom of God... In their view, the kingdom of God spoke of the reign and rule of God... This message of God's rule necessarily raised the issue of authority... At Christ's ascension and enthronement, he gave gifts to humanity, that is, the fivefold office ministries of apostle, prophet, evangelist, shepherd, and teacher, as delegated authorities for his kingdom rule.[49]

The 'rank, order, and authority' that Bevere talks about are an integral part of covering theology. Jerram Barrs writes that:

Some churches and Christian communities have built their authority on an exalted view of the church... With such a view it is easy for an authoritarian form of government to develop, for those at the head of the pyramid...are seen as Christ's representatives on earth.[50]

This pyramidal view of the Church is seen throughout *Under Cover*. There can only be one top to a pyramid, and Bevere contends that there is a biblical precedent to see one man in a leadership position in a church. After a brief reference to Moses, (how Bevere uses the Old Testament will be discussed later), Bevere says that

---

[49] Moore, *Shepherding*, 69-70.

[50] Jerram Barrs, *Shepherds & Sheep: A Biblical View of Leading and Following* (Downers Grove: InterVarsity Press, 1983), 42.

'James was the leader of the church in Jerusalem.'[51] To prove his statement, Bevere cites Acts chapter 15 and the decision of the council at Jerusalem regarding the issue of circumcision for new believers in Christ. Bevere summarises the incident as follows:

> *Some of the believing Pharisees who were also leaders spoke first. Then Peter spoke. After him, Paul and Barnabas shared what God was doing among the Gentiles. Once they had finished, James stood up, summarized what had been spoken, and then made this ruling, 'Therefore I judge...' As the head, he gave his decision, and all of them, including Peter, Paul, and John, submitted to his decision.[52]*

Other scriptures that Bevere uses to prove the headship of James are Acts 12:17 when Peter, after being miraculously delivered from prison by an angel, says to the believers at the house of Mary, 'Tell James and the brothers about this,' and Acts 21:17:18, in which Luke records Paul's arrival in Jerusalem: 'When we arrived at Jerusalem, the brothers received us warmly. The next day Paul and the rest of us went to see James and all the elders were present.' Bevere concludes from these scriptures that 'it is clear that he [James] was the lead man by the way he is separately mentioned by name.[53]

---

[51] Bevere writes, 'He [God] brought to my mind Moses. The Bible says, 'Moses certainly was faithful in the administration of all God's house.' He was the leader God put over the congregation.' Bevere, *Under*, 17.

[52] Ibid., 17.

[53] Ibid., 17.

The Jerusalem council scripture does indeed record James' words as 'Therefore, I judge...' However, this is very different from saying 'The judgement is...' James seems to have ended the debate and summed up the debate, but there *has* been debate and James does not make a final autocratic decision. Throughout the passage, we read of many contributions to the discussion:

> *Then some of the believers who belonged to the party of the Pharisees stood up...The apostles and elders met to consider this question. After much discussion, Peter got up and addressed them... The whole assembly became silent as they listened to Barnabas and Paul... When they finished, James spoke up... (Acts 15: 5-7, 12-13).*

Directly after James' sharing of his own judgment on the issue, we read: 'Then the apostles and elders, with the whole church, decided to choose some of their own men and send them to Antioch with Paul and Barnabas' (Acts 15:22). If this were a one-over-one theocracy, surely such a decision would have been made by James and not the 'whole church'? The actual letter to the Gentile believers is also recorded in the scripture, and the summary of the church is 'we all agreed to choose some men and send them to you with our dear friends Barnabas and Paul...' (Acts 15:25). A consensus is clearly shown, and not a one-man leader who makes the final decision himself.[54]

Andrew Walker's succinct phrase for the sort of system that Bevere is advocating is 'a Charismatic episcopacy.'[55] The latter part of the phrase indicates, of course, that such a system is not particularly new: there have been many church polities that have sought to arrange authority - from polities that give all power to the people who sit in the pew, to polities that invest all power to a Pope who sits in his palace. However, as Jerram Barrs points out:

> *The traditional episcopal church guards the balance between the three houses of clergy, laity and bishops so that careful checks and balances limit all human authority.*[56]

Ironically, Derek Prince uses the passage about the Jerusalem Council to argue *against* the one-man model of ministry. He writes of the gift of 'ruling' mentioned in Romans 12:8 but comments:

> *...once the basic plurality of leadership in the church has been established, the Holy Spirit will normally impart to one of the leaders this charisma for 'ruling' - a special gift for*

---

[54] Bevere's position is exactly the same as Watchman Nee's who writes: 'Peter and Paul only related facts, but James made the judgment. Even among the elders or apostles there was an order.' [Nee, *Authority*, 69]. It is ironic that classical Presbyterianism uses incidents such as that recorded in Acts 15 to practise the formation of presbyteries and synods consisting of all the elders from different congregations. Hardly a one-man model of leadership!

[55] Andrew Walker, *Restoring the Kingdom: the Radical Christianity of the House Church Movement* (Guildford: Eagle, 1998), 147. Walker's phrase is actually directed at the UK Restorationist movement of the 1970s and 1980s.

[56] Barrs, *Shepherds*, 41.

administration and direction within the collective leadership. It will not necessarily be permanent.[57]

For Prince, the conference in Jerusalem was where 'the charisma of leadership rested upon James. However, the final decision...was a unanimous decision of the whole group.'[58] Frank Viola argues that 'the very ethos of the New Testament militates against the idea of a single pastor... No church in the first century had a single leader.'[59] In regarding decision making, Viola argues that the New Testament method is 'neither dictatorial nor democratic. It was consensual. And it involved all the brothers and sisters.'[60] His summary reads:

> *All in all, the New Testament knows nothing of an authoritative mode of leadership. Nor does it know a 'leaderless' egalitarianism. It rejects both hierarchical structures as well as rugged individualism. Instead, the New Testament envisions leadership as coming from the entire church... Elders were called to exercise pastoral oversight in the context of mutual subjection rather than in a hierarchical structure of subordination.*[61]

---

[57] Prince, *Discipling*, 15.

[58] Ibid., 15.

[59] Viola, *Reimagining*, 170, 173.

[60] Ibid., 171.

[61] Ibid., 199.

The New Testament consistently teaches a plurality of elders over each local congregation: '...appoint elders in every town, as I directed you...' (Titus 1:5); 'Paul and Barnabas appointed elders for them in each church...' (Acts 14:23); 'From Miletus, Paul sent to Ephesus for the elders of the church,' (Acts 20:17); 'To all the saints in Christ Jesus at Philippi, together with the overseers and deacons,' (Phil 1:1). In 1 Tim 5:17, Paul writes that 'the elders who direct the affairs of the church well are worthy of double honour, especially those whose work is preaching and teaching,' implying that there are some whose work is not in preaching and teaching.[62]

Teachers of covering theology often refer to the individual leadership of Old Testament figures. But, as Frank Viola says:

> *...those who point to the single leaders of the Old Testament to justify the single pastor system make two mistakes. First, they overlook the fact that all the single leaders of the Old Testament - Joseph, Moses, Joshua, David, Solomon, etc - were types of the Lord Jesus Christ, not a human officer. Second, they typically ignore the pattern for oversight that is clearly spelled out throughout the New Testament.[63]*

The New Testament oversight pattern may not be as 'clearly spelled out' as Viola contends, (witness the abundance of denominations), but a plurality of elders is certainly a New

---

[62] See also Acts 11:30, 15:2-6, 22-40, 21:17-18; 1 Thess 5:12-13; 1 Tim 4:14; Heb 13:7,17,24; 1 Pet 5:1-2; Jas 5:14.

[63] Viola, *Reimagining*, 174.

Testament pattern. Bevere's arguments for a one-man model of leadership may have been argued with the noblest of intentions. The ubiquitous individualism of contemporary Western society is a fact, and order not chaos is to be seen in the church (as is the process of discipling to reach Christian maturity). Whatever the intentions, however, the argument is not scriptural.

The hierarchical model is essential in covering theology and firmly espoused in Bevere's book. With God as the source of all authority, this authority then trickles down to his delegated authority, and into the Church. The fivefold ministries of Ephesians chapter 4 are seen as offices of authority. The relevant passage reads:

> *It was he who gave some to be apostles, some to be prophets, some to be evangelists, and some to be pastors and teachers, to prepare God's people for works of service (Eph 4:11,12).*

Bevere writes:

> *The authority of the kingdom flows down through the offices... all authority was given to Jesus by the Father... Jesus in turn gave the fivefold ministries...His authority flows through appointed offices...We see an order of established authority.*[64]

Elsewhere Bevere asks us to look at Jesus' words in John 13:20. The text reads, 'I say to you, he who receives whomever I

---

[64] Bevere, *Under*, 184, 119.

send receives Me.' Bevere's chain of delegated authority through the Ephesians ministries is explained:

> *...the Father sent Jesus, and Jesus sends the fivefold ministers. If we receive His appointed ministers, we receive Him, and by receiving Him, we receive the Father. The chain of order does not stop with the fivefold ministers. It continues to those appointed by the ministers.*[65]

The most obvious thing to say about the passage in Ephesians, and Bevere's response to it, is that there is nothing in the text that shows that these offices are ordered here into a hierarchy. There is a case to be argued that none of the terms mentioned in Ephesians 4 are offices at all.[66] We do well to remember what the *purpose* of the apostles, prophets, evangelists, pastors and teachers is:

> *...to prepare God's people for works of service, so that the body of Christ may be built up until we all reach unity in the*

---

[65] Ibid., 127.

[66] It might be argued that the role of 'Apostle' suggests an office, with Judas Iscariot's position in this role having to be filled (Acts 1:21). However, the New Testament clearly mentions more than the 12 Apostles in the early church. Prophets and evangelists seem to abound, with no mention of an 'official/office' role. And, as some commentators have pointed out, if 'prophets' are second in hierarchy why weren't they part of the Jerusalem council? Why are only apostles and elders mentioned at this pivotal meeting? Lastly, the word 'pastor' isn't used to describe either a role or a position within the church anywhere else in scripture.

faith and in the knowledge of the Son of God and become mature, attaining the full measure of perfection found in Christ' (Eph 4:12- 13).

The terms are non-hierarchical: 'God's people', 'the body of Christ', 'unity in the faith.' With such a strict view of authority and delegated authority, Bevere's *Under Cover* is at odds with the biblical proposition that we are a priesthood of believers in Christ. Relationships with the body of Christ are not vertical but horizontal.

Bevere's position on authority and office only makes sense if we adhere to his literal concept of the kingdom of God being a kingdom in the here and now, with God as King, and with delegated authority expressed in rank, order, status, position, office, etc. Bevere's semantics might be more biblical than the Salvation Army, whose titles are taken from a secular army, but is the ecclesiology behind the terminology correct? Howard Snyder argues the following:

> *The church must seek its direction and authority, not primarily in leadership structures, but in the authority of Scripture interpreted by the collective sensitivity and maturity of the **whole** body of Christ - the whole Christian universal priesthood - guided by the Holy Spirit... the issue at stake in current abuses of shepherding and eldership is the New Testament doctrine of the priesthood of believers.*[67]

---

[67] Barrs, *Shepherds*, 9.

The biblical concept of the priesthood of believers is not only seen in the scriptures 1 Pet 2:9 and Rev 1:5-6 but in the biblical image of the Church as the Body of Christ with all members needed and equally important (1 Cor 12). All members are equal (Gal 3:26-29) and all have the same access to God (Heb 4:14-16; 1 John 2:1-2). The title of 'priest' for the believer in Jesus means direct access to God for that same believer. Authority structures such as those advocated by Bevere tend to obstruct this direct access and are, in effect, a throwback to the pre-Reformation Western church. Frank Viola argues that the Reformers didn't go far enough. He says:

The Reformation recovered the truth of the priesthood of all believers. But it failed to restore the organic practices that embody this teaching. The Reformation view of the priesthood of all believers was individualistic, not corporate. It was restricted to soteriology and didn't involve ecclesiology.[68]

Covering theology causes a new form of Christian priesthood to emerge. Bevere is quite explicit that leaders have direct access to God in a way that 'ordinary' non-leaders do not. They are, after all, God's delegated authority, next in the authoritative chain from the ultimate authority (God) to the rest of the world and to the Church. This is seen most clearly in Chapter 12 of *Under Cover*. The author mentions a time in his life when, as a church worker, he thought the

---

[68] Viola, *Reimagining*, 58. In contrast, Bevere operates with a sort of 'spiritual CEO' model where the organisation / church is led by command.

decisions of his pastor to be unwise and 'murmured in my heart against them.'[69] He then reveals that 'one day the Spirit spoke to me, *I have a question for you.*'[70] There then follows a dialogue between Bevere and the Holy Spirit:[71]

> ***Did I put you in the position of pastor, or did I put him in the position of pastor?*** *I said, 'You put him in the position.' The Lord quickly said,* **That is right. Therefore, I will show him things I don't need to show to you, and many times I will keep the wisdom of his decision from you on purpose, to see if you will follow him as he follows Me.**[72]

Bevere goes on to say that it would always be the case, usually months later, when the wisdom of the pastor's decision would surface. He concludes that 'God did not limit our submission to authorities to the times when we see their wisdom, agree with them, or like what they tell us. He just said, 'Obey!'[73] He then attributes the following words to God:

> *Later the Lord spoke to my heart,* **John, if I intended for**

---

[69] Bevere, *Under*, 146.

[70] Ibid., 146.

[71] The words that Bevere attributes to the Holy Spirit are always represented in bold form in this text.

[72] Bevere, *Under*, 146.

[73] Ibid., 147.

every believer to get all his information, wisdom, and direction only from prayer and communion with Me, then I'd never have instituted authority in the church. I placed authorities in the church with the full intent that My children could not get all they needed just from their prayer life. They would have to learn to recognise and hear My voice through their leaders as well.[74]

This methodology of invoking the voice of God in the teaching of *Under Cover* does not place the author beyond criticism. It is an astonishing claim to say that God Himself revealed to Bevere that He was not all-sufficient for the believer. A similar claim of the essentiality of leaders for the believer is given using Korah's rebellion. The rebellion and opposition to Moses and Aaron from Korah, Dathan, Abiram and On, along with 250 Israelite men, is given in Numbers 16. We read:

They came as a group to oppose Moses and Aaron and said to them 'You have gone too far! The whole community is holy, every one of them, and the LORD is with them. Why then do you set yourselves above the LORD's assembly?'(Num 16:3).

Bevere analyses the passage as follows:

You've heard it before! If not these exact words, then definitely the message is frequently portrayed by behaviour

---

[74] Ibid., 147.

or subtler words, but it's still the same spirit. You may hear, 'We're all equal' or 'We're all brothers and sisters' or 'We all have the Holy Spirit; why should we have to submit to their leadership?' These people are convinced they can hear the Lord as well as anyone else can.[75]

This claim that church leaders mediate between God and men is not New Testament teaching.

---

[75] Ibid., 187.

CHAPTER FIVE

THE OLD TESTAMENT IN BEVERE'S THOUGHT

The word 'priest' resonates with Old Testament narrative and imagery, and Bevere frequently uses the Old Testament in his teaching. The figure of the church pastor as an Old Testament prophet or priest is a common symbolic image in some forms of Pentecostalism. The church pastor is the leader, the anointed one, who leads his people into the promised land of Christ's blessings. But drawing theological propositions from the Old Testament is fraught with difficulties. There is, as one commentator puts it, 'a substantial discontinuity between the ways God established for Israel and the fact that there has been a tremendous change under the New Covenant inaugurated by the Christ Event.'[76]

In commenting on the Restoration / House Church movements in the UK during the 1970s and 1980s, Andrew Walker also comments on the 'elaborate use of typology and Old Testament incidents which are then read into the New Testament and the present day.'[77] Walker concludes that the most effective use of Old Testament typology for the Restoration movement in the UK was to compare the kingship of Saul and David with the state of leadership in the Church:

---

[76] Sawyer, "Obedience," n.p.

[77] Walker, *Restoring*, 88.

It was pointed out that Saul was not ordained by God but was chosen by the people. Democratic methods were compared unfavourably with the theocratic arrangements of God.[78]

There is no attention given at all in *Under Cover* to the question of ordination or of how leaders are actually chosen. Throughout the book, Bevere assumes his audience to be a man or woman who needs to be in submission to a church leader. Conversely, there is a definite focus, as Andrew Walker recognised in Restorationism, to many of the Old Testament typologies.

The story of David and Saul is commonly used by teachers of covering theology. It is said that the attitude and actions of David towards Saul provide an example of how to honour the office and not the man. The incidents in which David had the opportunity to kill Saul are said to show David's submission; and the killing of the Amalekite who killed a dying Saul is also cited. However, as Bob Buess points out:

The truth of the matter is, David did not honour Saul. He did not submit to the office either. He gathered an army of men about him to protect himself from Saul and his office as king. He humiliated Saul on two different occasions, once by taking his sword and again by cutting off his coat tail. He ran from him rather than submit. If he had submitted, he would

---

[78] Ibid., 88.

have been killed by Saul.[79]

Moses is also portrayed as an example for a New Testament leader. Bevere discusses the grumblings of the people against Moses. In Numbers chapter 20 we have an account of Moses falling into authoritarian excess. Walter Chantry says that 'the outstanding flaw of Moses on this occasion was thrusting himself into the foreground. His statement was one of personal hurt and self-defence, 'Must we bring you water out of this rock?' Moses failed to 'sanctify the Lord God in their sight.'[80]

Watchman Nee trod a similar path in viewing Moses as a lesson for the New Testament Church. In commenting on the Hebrews' grumbling regarding Moses and Aaron, he writes:

Whenever man touches God's delegated authority he touches God within that person; sinning against delegated authority is sinning against God... The people thought they were merely opposing Moses and Aaron; they had not the slightest intention of being rebellious to God, for they still wished to serve him. They were merely scornful of Moses and Aaron. But, God and his delegated authority are inseparable. It is not possible to maintain one attitude towards God and another attitude towards Moses and Aaron. No one can reject God's delegated authority with one hand and receive

---

[79] Bob Buess, *Discipleship Pro and Con* (Texas: Buess, 1975), 39.

[80] Roger Beardmore, ed., *Shepherding God's Flock: Essays on Leadership in the Local Church* (Harrisonburg, VA: Sprinkle, 1988), 193.

God with the other hand. If they would submit themselves to the authority of Moses and Aaron they would then be in subjection to God.[81]

This 'inseparable' aspect of God from his delegated authority (God from a human leader) is commented on by Bevere:

These men and women thought their insubordination was against Moses and not in any way connected to God. They thought they had successfully separated the two.[82]

Another use of the Old Testament that Bevere adopts is his paraphrase of Numbers 23:23. Bevere writes that the verse can read: 'There is no witchcraft that works against God's people, nor any divination against His Church!'[83] But, as *Under Cover* goes on to say, those outside the church and the 'covering' of its leaders are subject to, and in danger of, spiritual attack.

First Samuel chapter 15 details the disobedience of Saul to the prophet Samuel's request. Contrary to the express command from the prophet of God, Saul spared the life of the king of Amalek and also kept the best of the cattle alive. We read Saul's attempt at justifying his actions and Samuel's response:

Does the LORD delight in burnt offerings and sacrifices as

---

[81] Nee, *Authority*, 33, 36.

[82] Bevere, *Under*, 145.

[83] Ibid., 72.

much as in obeying the voice of the LORD? To obey is better than sacrifice, and to heed is better than the fat of rams. For rebellion is like the sin of divination, and arrogance like the evil of idolatry. Because you have rejected the word of the LORD, he has rejected you as king (1 Sam 15:22-23).

Bevere's interpretation of this reveals a very puzzling hermeneutic as well as a misunderstanding of how to translate biblical Hebrew into modern English. He writes:

Samuel directly linked rebellion with witchcraft: 'For rebellion is as the sin of witchcraft.' Notice the words 'is as' in this verse are in italic type. This is common in both the King James and the New King James Versions when words are used that did not appear in the original text. They were added later by the translators to lend clarity. A more accurate translation would have used only the word is.[84]

For Bevere, the Hebrew phrasing of 'For rebellion is witchcraft':

...clarifies the context of this scripture. It is one thing to liken rebellion to witchcraft, but an entirely different issue to say it is actually witchcraft. Obviously a true Christian would never knowingly practice witchcraft. But how many are

---

[84] Bevere cites Jay P. Green. The actual translation of this verse offered by Green puts the word 'is' in brackets, meaning Green's translation reads, 'For rebellion the sin of witchcraft.' Jay P. Green, ed., *The Interlinear Bible: Hebrew-Greek-English* (Peabody, MA: Hendrickson, 2005), 750.

under its influence unknowingly because of the deception of rebellion?[85]

A look at every other major Bible translation reveals that not one has rendered the passage to say that rebellion equals witchcraft. Three examples will suffice: 'For rebellion is like the sin of divination,' (New International Version); 'For rebellion is as the sin of divination,' (English Standard Version); 'For rebellion is as the sin of divination,' (New American Standard Version). It is hard to disagree with what one commentator has written:

> *I understand the temptation for pastors and authors to cherry pick translations that best suit the point they are trying to make. What Bevere does here isn't so innocent. He is ignoring what the church plainly knows. It is dishonest for someone with no training in interpreting Hebrew or Greek to claim that every single modern translation of a particular passage is wrong.*[86]

There is a standard interpretation of this passage: Saul did not realise how serious his mistake was and Samuel was pointing out to Saul how serious it actually was by comparing it to other things that Saul would consider serious. Clarification of this verse's context would take into account the basic facts that Saul was the king of

---

[85] Bevere, *Under*, 67.

[86] Tebay, "Covering," n.p.

Israel who was disobeying explicit instructions from a prophet of the God of Israel. In other words:

> *Covering theology attempts to equate God's direct command to Saul to the relatively minor decisions of a church leader. The two don't carry the same weight.*[87]

Tyumura reminds us that both verses 22 and 23 of this chapter 'constitute poetic prose, which exhibits characteristic features of parallelism.'[88] There is consensus among biblical scholars (and Bible translators) that when a simile is used in biblical Hebrew, the two words are placed together with no words in-between. An English translation needs to add 'as is' or 'is like' to make sense. Tyumura also cites Baldwin's interpretive summary which has nothing to do with how a believer relates to a church leader:

> *...no ceremonial can make up for a rebellious attitude to God and his commandments, because obstinate resistance to God exalts self-will to the place of authority.*[89]

Bevere's peculiar translation will surely cause fear for the Christian who believes in covering theology. Bevere teaches the

---

[87] Ibid., n.p.

[88] David Toshio Tsumura, *The First Book of Samuel* (NICOT; Grand Rapids: Eerdmans, 2007), 401.

[89] Tsumura, *Samuel*, 401.

Christian that 'witchcraft directly opens one to the demonic realm,' and that there can be 'total ignorance of what one is doing to complete understanding and awareness of the powers of darkness involved.'[90] For Bevere, the sin of witchcraft equals the sin of rebelling against God, which equals the sin of rebelling against his delegated authority. And, 'in essence witchcraft can be practised either with total unawareness or with complete knowledge.'[91] In talking anecdotally about his contact with those who have been involved in the occult, Bevere writes of how witchcraft covens initiate individuals by encouraging them to rebel. He summarises:

> *They are taught the more you rebel, the more power you obtain, and they seek power. This is true because rebellion is witchcraft. The more they rebel, the more they give legal access to demonic powers to influence, control, and empower their lives. By rebelling against the order and laws of God and His delegated authority, they knowingly grant legal access to the controlling demonic realm.*[92]

The story of Saul's rejection as king over Israel, as a result of the disobedience with the Amalekites and their cattle, leads on to the familiar narrative of David's sojourn in the wilderness to preserve his life as Saul is intent on ending it. Teachers of covering theology use this story in an attempt to convince believers that they should

---

[90] Bevere, *Under*, 67.

[91] Ibid., 68.

[92] Bevere, *Under*, 68.

remain submitted to their teachers/pastors/church leaders even if we are suffering under this authority. First Samuel 24 has Saul pursuing David with three thousand men to the desert of En Gedi. We read:

> *He [Saul] came to the sheep pens along the way; a cave was there, and Saul went in to relieve himself. David and his men were far back in the cave. The men said, 'This is the day the LORD spoke of when he said to you, 'I will give your enemy into your hands for you to deal with as you wish.' Then David crept up unnoticed and cut off a corner of Saul's robe. Afterwards, David was conscience-stricken for having cut off a corner of his robe. He said to his men, 'The LORD forbid that I should do such a thing to my master, the LORD's anointed, or lift my hand against him; for he is the anointed of the LORD.' (1 Sam 24:3-6).*

The misinterpretation of this passage, that covering teaching embodies, sees in David's refusal to kill Saul an example of biblical submission.[93] However, it is clear that for David 'touching the LORD's anointed' simply means not physically harming the king of Israel. A few verses later in the chapter, David calls out to Saul '…the LORD gave you into my hands in the cave. Some urged me to kill you, but I spared you; I said, 'I will not lift my hand against my master, because he is the LORD's anointed' (1 Sam 24:10).

The story of David fleeing and Saul pursuing actually shows

---

93 Ibid., 169-175.

a *lack* of submission from David to the king. David also instructed the king's son, Jonathan, to lie to his father. He became the leader of four hundred men 'who were in distress or in debt or discontented' (1 Sam 20:6-7; 22:2). Such a group of malcontents, disobeying their king by not surrendering their leader, is hardly the pretext to teach biblical submission as Bevere sees it; nor are the rest of the Old Testament typologies fitting examples to use in teaching about relationships within the New Testament Church of God.

CHAPTER SIX

SUFFERING IN BEVERE'S THOUGHT

One thing that can certainly be said about David is that he suffered under an unreasonable leader. This is an essential part of Bevere's teaching in *Under Cover*. If a believer remains submitted to an unreasonable leader, they will inherit God's blessing through that leader because of their own submission. Bevere begins this argument by saying that in the opening chapters of 1 Samuel, Hannah (the soon-to-be mother of Samuel) was blessed by the words of the priest Eli because she responded to his error of discernment in respect. As Hannah is praying for a child 'in bitterness of soul' we read:

> *As she kept on praying to the LORD, Eli observed her mouth. Hannah was praying in her heart, and her lips were moving but her voice was not heard. Eli thought she was drunk and said to her, 'How long will you keep on getting drunk? Get rid of your wine' (1 Sam 1:12-14).*

Bevere then interprets Eli's mistake as showing that he was 'insensitive to her pain...spiritually numb...a fleshly, insensitive priest.'[94] He gives his own modern-day example of Hannah's travail in Jerusalem:

---

[94] Bevere, *Under*, 115. This eisegesis results in character assassination. We only learn in chapter 2 of 1 Samuel that it is Eli's *sons* who are wicked. Once Eli hears of this he rebukes them. Although Eli is rebuked by a prophet, the biblical record shows none of the attributes Bevere gives to him. Eli is still entrusted to raise up Samuel to hear the Lord.

How would you have responded if your pastor had accused you of evil at the moment of your greatest pain? Perhaps you would have thought, **This guy is the head pastor? Doesn't he know I am fasting and crying out to God? What an insensitive, unspiritual jerk! This is the last time I will come here to worship!**[95]

For Bevere, the focus is on Hannah's reaction to Eli's mistake: a mistake he is at pains to stress is hurtful, insensitive, fleshly and unspiritual. Bevere cites Hannah's denial, and summarises:

She responded with respect and honour. Even though his actions and assessment far from deserved it, she honoured the position of authority on his life...If anything was wrong with the leader, God would deal with it.[96]

Bevere says that the blessing of Samuel was a response to her submission to her church leader: 'God used a fleshly, insensitive priest to release the words to bring forth the conception of a promise. A closed womb was opened, and life came out of darkness.[97] The behaviour of the leader is irrelevant compared to the fact of his office.[98] Bevere says:

---

[95] Ibid., 114.

[96] Ibid., 115.

[97] Ibid., 115.

[98] Although Bevere *does* say 'blatant corruption or sin' means we 'should not continue to drink from his defiled fountain.' Bevere, *Under*, 117.

...when God places His authority on a person, no matter his private or personal behaviour, we may still receive if we look beyond it and honour him as sent from God...Hannah knew what Jesus later confirmed, 'Most assuredly, I say to you, he who receives whomever I send receives Me; and he who receives Me receives Him who sent Me.'[99]

First Samuel 1:9-20 shows that it was Hannah's submission to God, and not to any leader or office, which gave her the blessing. Hannah is praying to God, and making vows to God. The priest Eli, upon realizing she is not drunk, says 'May the God of Israel grant you what you have asked of him,' (1 Sam 1:17). We are told that when Elkanah slept with Hannah 'the LORD remembered her' and, of course, the very name Samuel means 'heard of God.' Hannah testifies that his name is Samuel 'because I asked the LORD for him' (1 Sam 1:20). Similarly, her prayer of thanksgiving in 1 Samuel chapter 2 does not mention the priest Eli - she thanks God for the blessing she is to receive.

Such is the pivotal place of 'delegated authority' in covering theology that the Biblical story of God blessing Hannah with Samuel becomes the story of God blessing Hannah with Samuel because she obeyed a leader - and, in Bevere's view, an unspiritual, insensitive and fleshly one.

Bevere's focus on the less-than-perfect behaviour of Eli,

---

[99] Ibid., 116.

corresponds to a lack of focus on the character and godly qualities of church leaders in *Under Cover*. Instead the focus is on their office and the subsequent demands on believers to submit to that office. Both the example of David with Saul, and Hannah with Eli, are used by Bevere to promote submission to the office of a church leader no matter what their personal qualities or characteristics may be. The New Testament, however, exhorts us to subject ourselves to one another - 'Submit to one another out of reverence for Christ' (Eph 5:21). We are to subject ourselves in love to those who have displayed noble character and sacrificial service.[100]

Chapter 13 of *Under Cover* is titled 'Unfair Treatment' and in it Bevere writes:

> *Spiritual authority is promised to those who suffer like Christ. The greater hardship you endure, the greater the authority God entrusts to you. Again, you see that God sets you up for a blessing when you encounter unreasonable authority. But will you respond correctly and receive the blessing, or will you become resentful and bitter?[101]*

If a believer suffers under an unjust leader and responds correctly (submit and obey) they will receive a blessing. Added to this, Bevere teaches that God judges a believer on how faithfully they followed authority and not on the fruit of their life. After

---

[100] See, for example, 1 Cor 16:10-11, 15-18; Phil 2:29-30; 1 Thes 5:12-13; 1 Tim 5:17; Heb 13:17.

[101] Bevere, *Under*, 177.

pointing out the truth that 'leaders will be judged for their decisions,' Bevere goes on to write about 'our judgment' in relation to that of leaders:

> *On the other hand, our judgment will be relative to our submission, for authority is of God. To resist delegated authority is to resist God's authority. We should not take upon ourselves the pressure to discern beforehand whether leaders are right or not. Nor should we judge after the fact. This is not our burden, but God's. He alone knows and can change hearts as He so desires.[102]*

The teaching is exactly the same as that found in Watchman Nee, who says in *Spiritual Authority*:

> *People will perhaps argue, 'What if authority is wrong?' The answer is, if God dares to entrust his authority to men, then we can dare to obey. Whether the one in authority is right or wrong does not concern us, since he has to be responsible directly to God. The obedient needs only to obey; the Lord will not hold us responsible for any mistaken obedience, rather will he hold the delegated authority responsible for his erroneous act. Insubordination, however, is rebellion, and for this the one under authority must answer to God.[103]*

Bevere's chapter 'Unfair Treatment' begins with the message

---

[102] Ibid., 147.

[103] Nee, *Authority*, 71.

that God's goal for each of us as a believer is to 'break us'. He cites Psalm 34, 'The LORD is near to those who have a broken heart, and saves such as have a contrite spirit' (Ps 34:18), and Psalm 51:

> *For You do not desire sacrifice, or else I would give it; You do not delight in burnt offering. The sacrifices of God are a broken spirit, a broken and a contrite heart - these, O God, You will not despise (Ps 51:16-17).*

For Bevere, however, this 'broken heart' which is a 'prerequisite for intimacy with the Lord'[104] is linked with a broken will in relation to submission to authority. Bevere even uses the analogy of a warhorse:

> *A warhorse is not fit for service until his will is broken.... To be broken does not mean to be weakened. It has to do with submission to authority... As with horses, our breaking process deals with our response to authority. God customizes the perfect process for each of us, and this always entails some form of leadership.[105]*

The original meaning of being broken before the Lord himself, has itself been broken and moulded into being broken before the will of God's delegated authority - the human leader or pastor. In fact, Bevere will use the biblical injunction of 1 Peter as an instruction for church members to submit to church leaders. The

---

[104] Bevere, *Under*, 160.

[105] Ibid., 161.

scripture says:

> *Therefore submit yourselves to every ordinance of man for the Lord's sake... Servants, be submissive to your masters with all fear, not only to the good and gentle, but also to the harsh (1 Pet 2:13,18).*

Bevere explains that he will put this in 'modern vernacular':

> *Servants could be identified as employees, students, church members, or civilians. Masters could be employers, teachers, church leaders, or governmental leaders....God commands us to be submissive not only to the good and gentle, but also to the harsh![106]*

Bevere then selects three other translations of the same passage. The New Century Versions reads, 'Not only those who are good and kind, but also those who are dishonest'; the Contemporary English Version has, 'Do this, not only to those who are kind and thoughtful, but also to those who are cruel'; while the New American Standard Bible says, 'Not only to those who are good and gentle, but also to those who are unreasonable.' According to Bevere, the Scriptures teach that a church member is to submit to a church leader even if that leader is harsh, dishonest, cruel and unreasonable. Bevere avoids the scriptural qualifications for church leaders entirely. There are two lists in the New Testament that describe the qualities that make one fit to be an elder. The Revised

---

[106] Ibid., 162.

Standard Version will be quoted and the first list is found in 1 Timothy:

> *Now a bishop must be above reproach, married only once, temperate, sensible, dignified, hospitable, an apt teacher, no drunkard, not violent but gentle, not quarrelsome, and no lover of money. He must manage his own household well, keeping his children submissive and respectful in every way; for if a man does not know how to manage his own household, how can he care for God's church? He must not be a recent convert, or he may be puffed up with conceit and fall into the condemnation of the devil; moreover, he must be well thought of by outsiders, or he may fall into reproach and the snare of the devil (1 Tim 3:1-7).*

The second list lies in Paul's letter to Titus and reads:

> *...appoint elders in every town as I directed you, men who are blameless, married only once, whose children are believers and not open to the charge of being profligate or insubordinate. For a bishop, as God's steward, must be blameless; he must not be arrogant or quick-tempered or a drunkard or violent or greedy for gain, but hospitable, a lover of goodness, master of himself, upright, holy, and self-controlled; he must hold firm to the sure word as taught, so that he may be able to give instruction in sound doctrine and also to confute those who contradict it (Titus 1:5-9).*

Author James W. Garrett points out that the two lists

'demonstrate that Paul was more concerned with character and temperament than he was with ability. Only two of the twenty listed traits refer to ability: all of the rest are character and temperament traits.'[107]

Bevere uses the example of Christ himself to encourage us to submit to authorities. Using the Amplified Bible's version of 1 Pet 2:21, 'For even to this you were called [it is inseparable from your vocation]. For Christ also suffered for you, leaving you [His personal] example, so that you should follow in His footsteps,' Bevere explains how the sufferings of Christ are our example:

> *How did he suffer? Peter had explained in the previous verse: unfair treatment from delegated authorities. At times, God places us in situations where we receive unreasonable treatment from authorities, as He did with David, Joseph, Daniel, the apostle Paul, and others. Our calling is to handle it correctly, and Jesus left us His personal example of how to do it.[108]*

Because Christ never defended himself before authorities, so likewise we should not defend ourselves before our authorities - i.e. church leaders. The link with 'divine covering' is made explicit:

---

[107] James W. Garrett, "New Testament Church Leadership in the Local Church," n.p. [cited 21 November 2011]. Online: http://www.doulospress.org/pprs.php. (Obtainable in 2012).

[108] Bevere, *Under*, 163.

Why didn't Jesus defend Himself? The reason: to remain under His Father's judgment and thus His protection... When we refuse to defend ourselves, we are hidden under the hand of God's grace and judgement... In contrast, those who defend themselves come under the jurisdiction of their accusers and their judgment and thus forfeit divine intervention.[109]

An obvious problem with using Jesus' relationship with the authorities of his day as our example is that Jesus was not always submissive to those in authority. Matthew's gospel details Christ's indignation and righteous anger with the religious authorities of His day: the Pharisees. He calls them 'hypocrites,' 'blind guides,' 'blind fools,' and 'children of hell' (Mat 23:13,15-17).

Again, Bevere's methodology of claiming a direct word from God to support his teaching is used - this time in a vision:

I recall a situation where I defended myself with one in authority over me. God afterward showed me a brief vision in my heart. I saw the Lord standing by me with His hands behind His back. He was refrained from bringing the aid I needed. Once I stopped justifying myself, He was at work on my behalf.[110]

Regarding the idea that Christians are judged according to

---

[109] Ibid., 164.

[110] Ibid., 164.

their submission to church leaders, Bevere has already asserted that God spoke directly to him during his time as a youth pastor. According to Bevere, the Holy Spirit said:

> *John, when you stand before Me in judgment for the time period that I have had you serve this pastor, you will not first give an account of how many youth you led to salvation in Orlando, Florida. You will first be judged on how faithful you were to the pastor I've put you under... In fact, you could win all the youth in Orlando and stand before Me and be judged for not submitting to and being faithful to the pastor I put you under.*[111]

Bevere's assertion that 'our judgment will be relative to our submission, for authority is of God,'[112] comes against manifold scriptures that directly contradict this. Scripture nowhere teaches that a Christian is judged by God according to how they submitted to delegated authority.[113]

Bevere ends the chapter with 1 Pet 3:18 and 4:1 - the exhortation that we are to arm ourselves for the similar sufferings Christ experienced, 'which in context of his epistle is unfair treatment from authorities.'[114] At one level this is true: Peter is

---

[111] Ibid., 18.

[112] Ibid., 147.

[113] See, for example, Eph 2:8,9; Rom 2:6; 1 Cor 3:10-17; John 15:5-6; Matt 7:18-20.

[114] Bevere, *Under*, 176.

writing to 'the exiles of the dispersion in Pontus, Galatia, Cappadocia, Asia, and Bithynia' (1 Pet 1:1), many of whom were undergoing various levels of persecution from authorities. However, these authorities (as in Romans 12) are civil or governing authorities. Peter's epistle is not written so that 'ordinary' members of the church of God should submit and not defend themselves against harshness from fellow believers who also happen to be church leaders / pastors / elders. The verse from Peter which instructs servants to be submissive to their masters goes on to ask, 'For what credit is it, if when you do wrong and are beaten for it you take it patiently?' (1 Pet 2:20). Bevere avoids this verse which talks of a physical beating from a master to a slave. Clearly, the contemporary culture of slavery, part of the social and historical context in which Peter is writing, is being referred to. For Bevere to add the words 'church employee' and 'church leader' to the terms 'servant' and 'master' is unjustifiable.

CHAPTER SEVEN

FAITH IN BEVERE'S THOUGHT

Bevere's penultimate chapter is called 'Great Faith' and teaches that the level of faith a believer has is linked with the level of his submission to a church leader. In essence, this is a natural outflow of the covering theology espoused. With God's delegated authority (the church leader) being God's representative for the believer, and with submission to God's delegated authority (the church leader) being the same as submission to God, all blessings - including faith - flow from God through the delegated authority to the believer. Bevere writes that 'the authority in which we walk is directly proportional to our submission to authority. The greater our level of submission, the greater our faith.[115]

With leaders representing God, any biblical parable or incident that talks of God's authority means that we can interpret such authority as the authority in a church leader. This is the case in Bevere's treatment of Christ's words concerning 'faith as small as a mustard seed' in Luke 17, and in the incident concerning the centurion's faith in Matthew 8. Bevere's interpretation of the passage in Luke 17 is detailed as a direct revelation from God.[116]

---

[115] Ibid., 214.

[116] Bevere writes, 'A few years ago I went into my office at 5:30am to pray as I'd done so many mornings before. Yet before I could begin, I heard the Holy Spirit's directive: *Go to*

The apostles say to Christ, 'Increase our faith!' to which he replies, 'If you have faith as small as a mustard seed, you can say to this mulberry tree, 'Be uprooted and planted in the sea,' and it will obey you,' (Luke 17:5-7).

Bevere explains that 'faith is given to each and every believer...We were allotted a measure of faith (Rom 12:3). This faith is in seed form, and it is our responsibility to cultivate and grow it. How does it grow?'[117] To answer this question, Bevere turns to the story of the servant in Luke 17. The servant performs his duties, 'the things that were commanded him' but the master in the story does not thank the servant – he has simply done what was expected of him. In his teaching, Christ then says 'So likewise you, when you have done all those things which you are commanded, say, 'We are unprofitable servants. We have done what was our duty to do'' (Luke 17:10). Bevere comments:

> *As I read, the words **done all** and **commanded** jumped off the page. Jesus connected this servant's obedience to his master with our obedience to God. In doing so He made three significant points related to increased faith.*[118]

Bevere's three points are that 'there is a direct connection

Luke chapter 17 and start reading from verse 5.' Bevere, *Under*, 210.

[117] Ibid., 211.

[118] Ibid., 212.

between faith and obedience to authority,' that 'faith increases only when we complete what we're commanded to do,' and that 'an attitude of true humility is of utmost importance.'[119] One can easily deduce, after the teaching on delegated authority, how easily a causal link can be then taught between obeying authority (i.e. a church leader), doing what is commanded (obedience) and displaying humility (not questioning a church leader and, if need be, suffering under a church leader). Bevere writes:

> *If you desire great faith, then obey God's authority, whether direct or delegated, all the way to completion. Your faith is directly proportionate to your obedience!*[120]

Not one scholarly commentator on these verses interprets Christ's teaching (most often known as 'The Parable of the Dutiful Servant') as a message on obeying church leaders. It is only if everything in Scripture is viewed through the prism of Bevere's interpretation of Romans 13 that such a conclusion can be reached. Bevere claims that the direct connection between faith and obedience is also seen in the account of the centurion in Matthew 8. When Christ enters Capernaum, a centurion asks him to help his servant. Jesus says he will come, but the centurion responds:

> *Lord, I do not deserve to have you come under my roof. But just say the word, and my servant will be healed. For I myself*

---

119 Ibid., 213.

120 Ibid., 220.

am a man under authority, with soldiers under me. I tell this one, 'Go,' and he goes; and that one, 'Come,' and he comes. I say to my servant, 'Do this,' and he does it (Matt 8:8-9).

Jesus is said to be astonished at the centurion's words, and responds with praise for his faith - 'I tell you the truth, I have not found anyone in Israel with such great faith' (Matt 8:10). As one commentator says, 'For millennia, Christian interpretation of this passage has centred around how the Centurion had so much faith that he didn't need Jesus to come into his house.'[121] For Bevere, and the proponents of covering theology, however, the key verse and message of the passage is in the centurion's words, 'For I also am a man under authority, having soldiers under me.' Bevere explains:

The Roman officer communicated to Jesus that he had the respect and submission of his soldiers because he was submitted to his commander. Therefore, he had the backing of the authority of his commander, who in turn had the backing of the authority of Rome... He said, 'For I also...' He recognised Jesus was a Servant of God under His kingdom's authority...The greatest faith Jesus encountered in more than thirty-three years on earth was not John the Baptist's or His mother Mary's....What made his faith so great? **Because he**

---

[121] Tebay, "Covering," n.p. Of course, the contrast between Jewish and Gentile faith is also seen here, as is the radical decision of Jesus to go to the house of a Gentile - (and a Roman centurion at that).

understood and walked in submission to authority.*[122]*

As one writer puts it, 'what weight hangs from so few words!'[123] Again, there is not one scholarly commentator who concludes that the passage teaches that faith increases if we obey our church leaders. The centurion's great faith is seen in that he believes Christ has the power to heal the sick person from a distance. Ron Burks summarises it well:

> *The central theme of this encounter is Jesus' recognition, in front of unbelieving Jews, of a Gentile's faith in God... This example is not support for a system of church authority, but is rather an encouragement for us to believe Jesus when he gives us his word. No military model of church government is supported by the New Testament.*[124]

Bevere's teaching is exactly the same as Derek Prince's in *Discipleship, Shepherding, Commitment.* Prince writes:

> *Because the centurion was the representative of the Roman emperor, forming part of a chain of command...every command he gave to a soldier or servant was invested with the emperor's authority... Thus, the centurion's statement, 'I also am a man set under authority,' sums up the scriptural*

---

122 Bevere, *Under*, 214 [bold type in this text represents italics in the original].

123 Tebay, "Covering," n.p.

124 Burks, *Damaged*, 136.

By arguing that there is a message in this passage about being submitted to our ultimate authority, and by using Imperial Rome or the 'delegated authority' of a church leader in this role, we have replaced Jesus as the ultimate authority.

Linked to this message of great faith being a fruit of great submission is Bevere's anecdotal teaching that submission to church leaders results in more miracles of healing. Citing John 1:11-12, 'He came to His own, and His own did not receive Him. But as many as received Him, to them He gave the right to become children of God,' Bevere writes of the 'fundamental truth' that this passage holds. This truth is that 'many times God will send us what we need in a package we don't want.'[126] Bevere links the 'presentation' or 'package' that God sent in Christ with the church leader. Just as Jesus said, 'You know neither Me nor my Father. If you had known Me, you would have known My Father also,' (John 8:19) so Bevere says that 'those who know the Father recognize His authority manifested in those He sends! It doesn't have to be explained, taught or proved.'[127] He records:

This explains why a minister can go to Africa and see blind

---

[125] Prince, *Discipleship*, 16.

[126] Bevere, *Under*, 121.

[127] Ibid., 122.

eyes opened, the disabled walk, and the deaf hear, then come to America and see only a few headaches or minor back problems healed. I could give numerous examples. In Africa, the man or woman is received as sent by God, no matter the appearance or packaging. Because the person is received and honoured this way, the precious African people are blessed by God's power and His presence. In America if the packaging is not just right, honour is withheld. It is proportional. To the degree you receive and honour the messenger as sent by God is the degree you receive from God through the person. Dishonour, and this will be your reception. Give great honour, and honour will be your portion.[128]

There is not one scholarly commentator or theologian who teaches that people can be healed if they submit to the church leader or healer. While a theology of healing may be complex and nuanced, what is certainly true is that the Scriptures nowhere suggest what Bevere explicitly teaches. Faith in God is always the prerequisite[129] and the 'gifts of healing' are given to the Church by the sovereign work of the Holy Spirit (1 Cor 12:9).

---

[128] Ibid., 122.

[129] See, for example, Mark 6:5; Luke 8:48; 9:41.

CHAPTER EIGHT

'OBEY YOUR LEADERS' IN BEVERE'S THOUGHT

In Chapter 15 of *Under Cover*, Bevere writes that the Christian is to remain submitted to a church leader even if that leader does not practise what he preaches. Christ says in Matthew 23 that 'the scribes and Pharisees sit on Moses' seat [of authority]. So observe and practise all they tell you; but do not do what they do, for they preach, but do not practice' (Matt 23:1-3 *Amplified Bible*). For Bevere, this shows that 'Jesus commanded submission even to corrupt leaders who didn't live what they preached. He pointed the multitudes to the authority upon them, not to their personal lives.'[130]

Did the early church obey the authority that was upon the Pharisees and religious leaders of their day? Are we taught in the Bible to always obey our church leaders? To answer this we must look at what might be called the lynchpin verse of covering theology and the Shepherding Movement - Hebrews chapter 13, verse 17. Bevere cites the New King James Version of this verse in Chapter 11 titled 'Obedience and Submission.' It reads:

> *Obey those who rule over you, and be submissive, for they watch out for your souls, as those who must give account. Let them do so with joy and not with grief, for that would be*

---

130 Bevere, *Under*, 206.

unprofitable for you (Heb 13:17).[131]

He explains the verse in this way:

The writer distinctly ordered us to do two things: (1) to obey those who rule over us; and (2) to be submissive to those who rule over us.[132]

There then follows an anecdote of a time when Bevere did not feel spiritually fed through the messages and teaching of the pastor he was working for at the time. He became critical of the pastor and was 'surrounded by friends who were as critical as I was.'[133] Again, there is direct revelation through the spoken voice of the Holy Spirit, a voice which teaches Bevere the difference between obedience and submission. With the divine voice italicized (in bold typeface here), Bevere writes of a meeting in which he sat listening to the pastor whom he had been so critical of:

As I was pondering my present starvation from not being fed, the Holy Spirit firmly informed me, **The problem is not with your pastor. The problem is with you!** *...You keep bringing*

---

[131] Ibid., 130. It is interesting that Bevere uses the New King James Version. Steven Lambert believes that 'one factor contributing to the excessive authoritarian interpretation of this verbiage is the rendering proffered by the Seventeenth Century translators commissioned by King James of England.' [Lambert, Captivation, 82]. Lambert reminds us of the historical context of the King James translation when state and religious rulers were one and the same, or at the least both ecclesiastical and state authority were sanctioned by each other.

[132] Bevere, *Under*, 131.

[133] Ibid., 132

up the lack of being fed. The book of Isaiah states, 'If you are willing and obedient, you shall eat the good of the land; but if you refuse and rebel, you shall be devoured by the sword' ...You obey everything you're told to do in this ministry, but I did not say, 'If you are obedient, you shall eat the good of the land,' I said, 'If you are willing and obedient.....' and willingness deals with your attitude. And your attitude stinks!...the reason you are not being fed (eating of the good of My kingdom) in this church is that though you are obedient, you are not willing![134]

Bevere then writes that his 'eyes were open,' he 'repented right away' and 'the heavens opened up, and I was astounded by the revelation God gave me through my pastor's teaching.'[135] His own teaching from the episode is given as the difference between obedience and submission:

When we are not submissive to our delegated authorities, we resist God's authority because they are appointed by Him! God wants us to be able to freely enjoy and benefit from the banqueting table He prepares for us through those He provides for us... Obedience deals with our responsive **actions** *toward authority. Submission deals with our* **attitude** *toward authority. This is where most of us miss it... For this reason the writer of Hebrews exhorted us not only to obey*

---

[134] Ibid., 132.

[135] Ibid., 134

those over us, but also to be submissive.[136]

Bevere uses the New International Version of Hebrews 13:17 ('Obey your leaders and submit to their authority') to ask, 'Where do we draw the line? Does God expect us to obey authorities, no matter what they tell us to do?'[137] The answer is:

> *The only time - and I want to emphasize the **only** exception in which we are not to obey authorities - is when they tell us to do something that directly contradicts what God has stated in His Word. In other words, we are released from obedience only when leaders tell us to sin...Whether the authority is civil, family, church, or social, God admonishes a submissive regard to be our attitude, and we are to obey in action, unless authority tells us to do what is **clearly** seen in Scripture as sin. Let me emphasize the word **clearly**...the believers did not obey when commanded to deny Christ, murder, worship other gods, or directly subvert a command of Jesus. They were not gray areas or judgment calls.*[138]

The first point that must be made concerning Heb 13:17 is that the New International Version inserts a word that is not a part of the Greek text. It says, 'obey your leaders and submit to their

---

[136] Ibid., 134.

[137] Ibid., 135.

[138] Ibid., 135.

authority.'[139] Without a knowledge of the original Greek, the reader would have no idea that the Greek word ἐξουσία which we translate as 'authority', is nowhere to be find in any ancient Greek manuscript. Other translations amend the New International Version's unfortunate addition: 'Obey your leaders and submit to them, for they are keeping watch over your souls...' (English Standard Version); 'Obey your leaders and submit to them, for they keep watch over your souls...' (New American Standard Bible).

Even without the word 'authority' the text obviously says that we should 'obey' and 'submit' to our leaders.[140] Again, knowledge of New Testament Greek reveals an important facet of the text. The Greek word which is translated 'obey' in the passage is πείθω which usually means 'persuade.'[141] One commentator has conceded that because of the way the word is used in the sentence, it can 'legitimately be translated 'obey' which is why most Bibles do,' but that the word 'still carries the nuance of obedience via persuasion rather than obedience to authority.'[142] This nuance is, of course, totally missing in the one word 'obey' which our English translations use. It should also be noted that the Greek form of πείθω used in the text is the present imperative middle form – πείθεσθε.

---

[139] It is strange that the latest revision of the New International Version (2011) now removes the word 'obey' but retains the addition of 'authority': 'Have confidence in your leaders and submit to their authority...'

[140] Bevere does not deal with the fact that the plural of 'leader' is used despite his attempts with the Jerusalem council to insist that the church always has one man as the leader.

[141] In fact, πείθω is the Greek goddess of persuasion, seduction and charming speech.

[142] Tebay, "Covering," n.p.

This gives the meaning 'permit oneself to be persuaded' or 'yield to persuasion.' Timothy Willis argues that πείθω should be translated 'be persuaded' and that translators have traditionally 'read a little too much Western Civilisation onto the text.'[143]

The passage does not exhort us to respect authority, nor does it mention delegated authority, nor does it teach blind obedience to any church leader or leaders. The rest of the passage points to persuasion. The Revised Standard Version reads:

> *Obey your leaders and submit to them; for they are keeping watch over your souls, as men who will have to give account. Let them do this joyfully, and not sadly, for that would be of no advantage to you (Heb 13:17).*

The reasons given for the believer to 'obey' or 'be persuaded' in regards to the leaders are that they are 'keeping watch over your souls'; they are people who 'will have to give account'; the believer is exhorted to 'let them do this joyfully'; and finally that not being persuaded by them 'would be of no advantage.' Nowhere are there warnings of not obeying God through not obeying God's delegated authority. And nowhere are there warnings or threats of spiritual deception or satanic attack if the leaders are not obeyed. Steven Lambert points out that:

---

[143] cited in Tebay, "Covering," n.p.

*...this Greek word translated **obey** in many English versions, **peitho**, is closely related to the word **pisteuo**, which means to trust...the difference in the meanings of the two words is that the **peitho** (persuasion-obedience) is produced by **pisteuo** (trust). In other words, the **obedience** spoken of here in the original language is more of a willing compliance and cooperation based on persuasion resulting from established trust and confidence.[144]*

Bevere does not include the other relevant portion of Hebrews 13 which occurs just ten verses prior. Verse seven reads, 'Remember your leaders, who spoke the word of God to you. Consider the outcome of their way of life and imitate their faith' (Heb 13:7). The leaders who are to be remembered and who are yielded to joyfully are also the leaders with exemplary conduct and faith. The leaders' trust and ability to persuade is through merited esteem and not through any kind of positional office. John Calvin wrote:

...the apostle is only concerned with those who faithfully exercise their office. Those who have nothing except the title, and indeed those who abuse the title of pastor to destroy the Church, deserve little reverence and even less faith. The apostle says this expressly in saying that they watch for your souls, because this does not apply to any except those who are true rulers, and who are in fact what they are called. The

---

[144] Lambert, *Captivation*, 80.

papists who use this as a foundation for the tyranny of their idol are doubly foolish.[145]

Unlike Bevere, positional authority is not even acknowledged by Calvin. Instead, as in the requirements for eldership seen in 1 Timothy and Titus, character and conduct are all. Calvin was well aware that if positional authority were the ultimate authority, the whole Reformation was a rebellion against God's delegated authorities. Indeed, every Protestant denomination or church grouping (including Bevere's own church) is the spiritual descendant of somebody who has not obeyed a church leader.

There is another Greek word that is translated 'obey' and that word is πειθαρχέω. It is found in the account of Peter and the other apostles preaching the gospel despite the express command of the high priest. Acts 5:27-29 reads:

Having brought the apostles, they made them appear before the Sanhedrin to be questioned by the high priest. 'We gave you strict orders not to teach in this name,' he said. 'Yet you have filled Jerusalem with your teaching and are determined to make us guilty of this man's blood.' Peter and the other apostles replied: 'We must obey God rather than men!'

The word πειθαρχέω is used to refer to obedience to

---

[145] John Calvin, Hebrews and 1 & 2 Peter (CNTC 12; Grand Rapids: Eerdmans, 1994), 112.

magistrates or civil authorities but is never used when referring to church leaders. It is not the word that is used in Heb 13:17. It appears in Titus 3:1, 'Remind the people to be subject to rulers and authorities, to be obedient, to be ready to do whatever is good..' Again, the obedience is to civil magistrates and authorities and it is qualified by being ready to do 'whatever is good.' Blind obedience to any form of leadership or government is never an option if what is commanded is against the Word of God.

Not only are we encouraged to 'be persuaded by' our leaders in Heb 13:17, but we are also encouraged to 'be submissive.' The Greek word is ὑπείκω. Frank Viola reminds us that the Greek word most often translated 'submit' in the New Testament is ὑποτάσσω which is better translated 'subjection'. He writes of subjection being 'a voluntary attitude of giving into, cooperating with, and yielding to the admonition or advice of another,' which has 'nothing to do with control or hierarchical power' but is 'simply an attitude of childlike openness in yielding to others.'[146] Mary Alice Chrnalogar concurs and writes of the word used for 'submit' in Heb 13:17 by citing a popular reference tool for Bevere - Vine's Expository Dictionary of Biblical Words:

> *The word used here for 'submit' is HUPEIKO...[defined by Vine as] 'to retire, or withdraw.' The sense is one of 'yielding' or 'keeping out of the way' rather than 'following*

---

[146] Viola, *Reimagining*, 210-211.

an order.' The author of Hebrews is actually saying, 'Don't hinder or obstruct the leaders in doing their jobs, because they have to give an account to the Lord.'[147]

Bevere's interpretation of Heb 13:17 is of always obeying and submitting to church leaders with the 'only exception' being if they *'clearly'* direct us to sin - and the examples of sin he gives are the extremes of denying Christ, murdering and worshipping other gods. Hebrews 13:17 has been called 'the chestnut verse of the cults'[148] and, if Bevere's is the correct interpretation, one can see the reason behind its frequent citation from Shepherding and covering teachers. Astonishingly for an international Bible teacher who teaches covering, Bevere claims only a vague awareness of recent events in Charismatic church history. In the only paragraph of the entire book which mentions the modern Shepherding Movement he writes:

I understand that a movement within the church called discipleship got out of hand in the 1970s, and submission to leaders teetered out of balance. People were asking pastors about whether they could go on vacations, buy a specific car or other major item, or marry a certain individual. I wasn't involved so I don't know exactly how far overboard it actually went, but some who were involved said that it ended

---

147 Chrnalogar, *Twisted*, 43.

148 Vrankovich, "Leadership," n.p.

up being unscriptural.[149]

Such casual and unclear vagaries regarding recent church history contrast with Bevere's firm and clear revelation that we should always obey church leaders unless - and only unless - they are clearly commanding us to sin. Ironically, the three examples Bevere uses of the Shepherding Movement (where to holiday, what to buy, who to marry) are not examples of a church leader directing a believer to sin. But Bevere indicates, with no other explanation, that this is somehow 'out of balance' submission. No examples or further elaboration on the Shepherding Movement and its excesses is made.

The Greek word translated 'obey' in Acts 5:27-29 does not have the same connotations of 'be persuaded by' that are found in πείθω. Just as Luke does not give us an example of total obedience and submission to the religious authorities of the day, so Paul never teaches consistent obedience and submission to those in authority. In the second chapter of Galatians, Paul writes to the believers of his meeting with Christ's original apostles and the early church leaders:

Then after fourteen years I went up again to Jerusalem with Barnabas, taking Titus along with me...And from those who were reputed to be something (what they were makes no difference to me; God shows no partiality) - those, I say, who were of repute added nothing to me (Gal 2:1,6).

---

[149] Bevere, *Under*, 187.

No titles are used in Paul's reference to the very first leaders of the church in Jerusalem. Leighton Tebay comments:

It implies that the early government of the church followed the common traditional Jewish approach to leadership. There was a council of elders and apostles that was largely a group of equals. There would have been some who earned greater influence though their wisdom or experience but there was no hierarchy.[150]

Charles Cousar writes that Paul's repetition of the phrase 'those reputed to be something'[151] would seem to suggest 'a negative attitude toward the figures at Jerusalem as if Paul were sneering, at least slightly, at their prominence and place of esteem.'[152]

However, Cousar goes on to cite an article by David Hay which argues that Paul is not disparaging the early church leaders in this way:

He is simply telling the Galatians that decisions about apostles should not be made on external considerations (literally, 'God does not receive a person's face'). They should judge by reality (i.e., conformity of message and life to the gospel), not by appearance (i.e., mere rank). For

---

[150] Tebay, "Covering," n.p.

[151] The English Standard Version translates it as 'those who seemed to be important.'

[152] Charles B. Cousar, *Galatians: A Bible Commentary for Teaching and Preaching* (Kentucky: John Knox Press, 1982), 41.

himself, the status of the 'pillar apostles' was not so decisive that they could have dissuaded Paul from preaching the message of God's unconditional love for the Gentiles. But happily they did not try to do so.[153]

This same chapter of Galatians records Paul's challenge to Peter, one of 'the Twelve' no less. The challenge is public. It is clear that Paul is not afraid to question any leader on issues concerning the gospel and theological truth:

But when Peter came to Antioch I opposed him to his face, because he stood condemned... When I saw that they were not straightforward about the truth of the gospel, I said to Peter before them all (Gal 2:11,14).

A similar lack of submission and obedience (although which side is 'guiltier' is open to interpretation) is seen in Paul and Barnabas' disagreement in Acts chapter 15. The missionaries disagree over whether to take John called Mark with them. The Scripture records that 'there arose a sharp contention, so that they separated from each other; Barnabas took Mark with him and sailed away to Cyprus, but Paul chose Silas and departed...' (Acts 15:39-40). There is clearly no chain of command as advocated by Shepherding and covering teaching. In Bevere's theology, there would be one person who would clearly have the rank to make the decision and therefore one of the two (either Barnabas or Paul) is in

---

[153] Ibid., 42.

disobedience to God's delegated authority. Luke's inspired recording of the event, however, does not make any comment on such things. There is no teaching on why an apostle should be obeyed (nor is there any teaching on the consequences if you don't.) Instead, two separate ministries are formed over what might be termed an unfortunate human disagreement.

CHAPTER NINE

WHY DO PEOPLE GO 'UNDER COVER' AND REMAIN THERE?

Why do people follow and submit to teachers of covering theology? And why do teachers like Bevere insist that they are giving a greater measure of God's blessing into the Church by appropriating its concepts into the life of local fellowships? Bill Ligon, writing contemporaneously with the growth of the Shepherding Movement, talks of the natural search and need for 'place' within a Christian's life:

> *Problems in discipleship have developed because men have not understood this strong inner drive to find a place. Not realizing the consequences, many have bound themselves over to other people simply out of a need to be part of something or recognised by somebody.*[154]

William K. Kay writes of how the Shepherding Movement was a 'response to growing individualism and the directionless flow of the Charismatic movement.'[155] In talking of the extreme commitment that the Shepherding Movement birthed, Moore writes that there was a failure to realise this psychological need to belong to

---

[154] Bill Ligon, *Discipleship: The Jesus View. An Alternative to Extremism* (New Jersey: Logos International, 1979), 30.

[155] Kay, *Networks*, 195.

a group:

> *Many of the young people joining the movement had not been adequately parented and were looking for an authority figure to fill their need. The movement leaders did not understand the co-dependent dynamic in many people.*[156]

This is not the blanket answer for all who have been, or who are now a part of, an authoritarian church. Ron and Vicki Burks, who were in the Shepherding Movement from 1969 until 1988, write that 'there was no deep void in our souls that cried out for domination. For most of us it just wasn't that simple.'[157] In analysing their own reasons for remaining in the Shepherding Movement, they write of the committed relationships with like-minded believers that authoritarian churches often produce:

> *This committed relationship brings a great sense of security. There is the very real feeling, spiritually, of 'coming in out of the rain.' Those who share a commitment to the same pastor become close friends, and find commitment extending to one another.*[158]

In evaluating the reasons why Christians are happy to remain in churches that teach covering theology, one must also see a

---

[156] Moore, *Shepherding*, 75, 186.

[157] Burks, *Damaged*, 32.

[158] Ibid., 58.

reaction to the age in which we live, an age in which the authority of parents, teachers, and civil rulers is often held in contempt. Walter Chantry, pondering the fact that 'into many evangelical churches there has recently come an overbearing authority which is injuring the true flock of God,' asks whether an increase in such teaching is because our generation 'has been so unregulated by proper authority, those who seek to rule biblically now run to excesses.'[159] It is a sad fact that covering theology is attractive to some people as it fills a spiritual void. In exactly the same way that the Shepherding Movement attracted those who wanted more commitment and dedication in their Christian walk, so teachers of covering theology can attract zealous Christians who see a lack of accountability or leadership in their own local church.

What might be seen as a commendable zealousness contrasts sharply with another major motivation for those under the teachings of covering theology: fear. Throughout *Under Cover* there are anecdotes and explicit warnings that to come out from 'under cover' (i.e., to not obey your pastor) is to be at risk of satanic deception, demonic attack, financial instability, marital problems, and bitterness of spirit which stops all Christian growth. There is no Scripture used to back up such claims, nor can there be: nowhere in the Bible are we told that a Christian's submission to authority gives them spiritual protection. Leighton Tebay points out:

This isn't biblical submission because it isn't a voluntary

---

159 Beardmore, *Flock*, 184.

attitude of cooperation. This submission is involuntary because it is coerced by fears and threats. True accountability is the by product of true fellowship which is grounded in biblical freedom and motivated by love not fear.[160]

Even the subtitle of *Under Cover* shows the fear-based foundation in Bevere's covering theology: *The Promise of Protection Under His Authority*. If the reader believes that God's authority is manifest in the person of his or her church leader, then the obvious inference is that there is no promise of protection if we 'come out' from 'under' that authority. Bevere writes in Chapter 2:

> *If we attempt to live as believers with a cultural mind-set towards authority, we will be at best ineffective and at worst positioned for danger. Our provision as well as protection could be blocked or even cut off as we disconnect ourselves from the Source of true life.*[161]

This 'cultural mind-set' that Bevere warns us against is the democratic mind-set which is 'fine for the nations of the world' but is against God's kingdom principles of 'rank, order, and authority.'[162] Bevere cites Job in this chapter:

---

[160] Tebay, "Covering," n.p.

[161] Bevere, Under, 10.

[162] Ibid., 10.

If they obey and serve him, they will spend the rest of their days in prosperity and their years in contentment. But if they do not listen, they will perish by the sword and die without knowledge (Job 36:11-12).

We are asked to 'notice the promise: provision and protection in exchange for our submission to His authority,' and to also 'note the impending danger that accompanies our ignoring His government.'[163] This fear of impending danger is, of course, linked to submission to a church leader, for in the very next paragraph Bevere makes his claim that 'we cannot separate our submission to God's inherent authority from our submission to His delegated authority. All authority originates from Him!'[164]

We have already noted Bevere's wrong use of 1 Sam 15:22-23 and his warnings that 'witchcraft can be practised…with total unawareness,' that a Christian can be 'under its influence unknowingly because of the deception of rebellion,' and that 'by rebelling against the order and laws of God and His delegated authority…[people] grant legal access to the controlling demonic realm.'[165] In Chapter 7 of *Under Cover* (titled 'Bewitched') Bevere writes that the incident in Numbers 25, in which 24,000 Hebrew

---

163 Ibid., 11.

164 Ibid., 11.

165 Ibid., 68.

people died, 'affirms rebellion as witchcraft and grants *[sic]* legal entrance to demonic powers of control.' Bevere's interpretation of the event is that, as 'God is not the Author of plagues and diseases,' his 'covering of protection was lifted, and the enemy had legal access.' This was because 'the children of Israel blatantly rebelled and violated His authority.'[166] Bevere ignores the fact that Numbers 25 says that 'the LORD's anger burned against them' (Num 25:3).

Bevere claims that Gal 3:1 is a New Testament example of demonic powers being given 'legal access'. When Paul writes, 'O foolish Galatians! Who has bewitched you that you should not obey the truth…' (Gal 3:1) Bevere's explanation is that because of their disobedience 'Paul was telling the churches they were under a witchcraft curse!'[167] This explicit warning - not submitting to God's authority leads to satanic deception and a curse - will surely lead to a very real fear for many Christians that there is spiritual danger if they do not always obey their church leader. There is no scholarly interpretation of these verses that agrees with Bevere's view that the Christians in Galatia were literally under a curse because of disobedience. Rhetorical hyperbole is what is usually understood when looking at Gal 3:1. The apostle is exasperated and amazed that the Galatian Christians are forsaking their New Covenant gospel freedoms to be enslaved again to religious rules, laws and Old Covenant ceremonies (particularly circumcision).

---

[166] Ibid., 76.

[167] Ibid., 6. The Nestle-Aland / United Bible Societies' Greek text omits the words 'that you should not obey the truth.'

Another factor that causes Christians to continue to be a part of a church that teaches covering theology is the approach to Scripture that such churches typically take. It is a fact that both the Shepherding Movement and the impact and promulgation of teachings such as those in Bevere's *Under Cover* are almost exclusively seen in the Charismatic wing of the Church. Tebay writes of the 'fertile soil of the Charismatic church'[168] given its anti-intellectual and anti-scholarly bias. The scholarly historical/critical method of biblical interpretation is seen as spiritually dead and overly academic. Thus, a 'spiritually inspired' method of interpreting the Bible is used which, in effect, makes it very difficult to challenge the leadership or teachings of the church. With the leaders being God's delegated authority, they are also the ones with God's delegated interpretation of His Word. As Tebay writes:

> *If your 'covering' has more 'spiritual authority' than you, how do you know what is biblical and what isn't? How can scripture be used as leverage against unbiblical teaching when the highest authority isn't actually scripture, it is scripture rightly interpreted by God's delegated authority?[169]*

With the truths of God's Word needing spiritual discernment, and with the leaders of the church being invested with spiritual authority, the 'ordinary church member' is loath to challenge such a fixed set-up. Besides this, church members are not taught biblical

---

[168] Tebay, "Covering," n.p.

[169] Ibid., n.p.

hermeneutics, nor are they taught to think critically.

1 Samuel records the people of Israel demanding a king to rule over them. The direct governance of God in our lives is often an uncomfortable thought. We want a go-between or a mediator - or even a golden idol such as that made in Exodus 32. With perceptive psychological insight, Tebay says:

> *We want a tamer version of God as mediated through people. In covering theology people are not directly accountable to God. They are directly accountable to their human authority. These authorities are not so exacting and precise as a direct relationship with the Holy Spirit.*[170]

Tebay adds that while many people find the idea of submitting to another human being 'repugnant' there are others who 'shrink back from taking responsibility for their own actions and their own lives.'[171] For them, the safe attractions of a 'follow the leader' church are an integral part of their faith and walk with God. Frank Viola concurs:

> *The truth is that many of us - like Israel of old - still clamour for a king to rule over us. We want a visible mediator to tell us what 'God hath said'...The presence of a human mediator in a church is a cherished tradition to which many Christians are fiercely committed. But it doesn't square with Scripture...*

---

[170] Ibid., n.p.

[171] Ibid., n.p.

It suppresses the free functioning and full maturing of Christ's body.[172]

Leadership is power.[173] It involves the trust and respect of people. The preacher's communication skills and persuasive rhetoric while preaching the tenets of covering theology can undoubtedly sway the strongest mind. Though we may assume the advocates of covering are sincere, Johnson and Van Vonderen's text, *The Subtle Power of Spiritual Abuse*, points out that, sincere though preachers of wrong, abusive or authoritarian doctrines and practices may be, they are 'just as trapped in their unhealthy beliefs and actions as those who they knowingly or unknowingly abuse.'[174]

Despite the sincerity of some, there are surely those who knowingly teach covering theology to consolidate their power in the church. There are several instances in the Gospels in which Jesus' disciples are tempted to grasp after power,[175] while Peter instructs leaders not to 'lord it over' the church or domineer (1 Pet 5:1-5). What was a temptation for human nature then, is a temptation for human nature now.

---

[172] Viola, *Reimagining*, 163.

[173] Walter Chantry writes that 'refusal to think about the power connected with the Christian ministry is a variety of naïveté.' Beardmore, *Flock*, 190.

[174] David Johnson and Jeff Van Vonderen, *The Subtle Power of Spiritual Abuse: Recognising & Escaping Spiritual Manipulation and False Spiritual Authority Within the Church* (Minneapolis: Bethany House, 1991), 24.

[175] See Mat 18:1-4; 23:8-12; Mk 9:33-37; Lk 9:46-48; 22:24-27.

CHAPTER TEN

THE EFFECTS OF COVERING THEOLOGY AND CONCLUSIONS

Andrew Walker, writing in 1985, claimed that 'the evidence for the effects of shepherding is notoriously difficult to find.'[176] Twenty-five years later, can we see any obvious effects? The first element we can surely find is in the motivation for service that covering theology consistently evokes. True Christian servitude should be motivated by love for God and love for his people. In covering theology people are coerced or threatened with spiritual deception if they do not always obey God's delegated authority found in the church leader. Spiritual legalism and fear can be the main controlling factors for Christian obedience. The elders and leaders in churches which teach covering theology will, due to the theology itself, rarely be held accountable: a precarious state of affairs. Those who voice contrary opinions can be labelled as rebellious or in deception. As Walter Chantry says, 'to categorise certain Christians as enemies or the tools of Satan will not build up God's kingdom, but it will create an attitude of paranoia' which can 'destroy the spiritual health of the church' and can even lead to 'cult-like excesses.'[177] In trusting that 'leadership knows best' and that, as leaders, they are at the top of the

---

[176] Walker, *Restoring*, 153. Walker does go on to say that 'it would seem likely that paternalism breeds dependency, and shepherding, instead of producing Christian leaders, merely produces sheep.'

[177] Beardmore, *Flock*, 195.

pyramid and therefore know God better, critical thinking is sapped away. Allowing others to make decisions for them leaves the Christian as a spiritual infant. The fruit of the Holy Spirit in self-discipline, and mature decision making with 'the mind of Christ' is lost. One writer says that 'leaders should be eager to foster independence and internal moral control in their members, avoiding dependency.'[178] And, as Walter Chantry notes, the spiritual pedigree of the church in future generations will be damaged. If the church leader or elders are authoritarian then men of strong minds and independent judgment will leave the church - 'these very ones would have the greatest potential for future leadership in the assembly.'[179] Bob Buess agrees with this assessment when he writes of the 'neo-discipleship' movement - his term for the Shepherding Movement:

> *Following the neo-discipleship route the strong individuals are destroyed. Men with deep convictions must submit them to the shepherd... It promotes 'yes men'. The neo discipleship doctrine and dogma rules out men of convictions. This does away with men who hear from God. This, in reality, kills the move of God.[180]*

---

[178] Dennis McCallum, "Leadership and Authority in the Church: What It Is and Isn't," n.p. [cited 21 November 2011]. Online: www.xenos.org/classes/leadership/leadershipandauth.html (Obtainable in 2012).

[179] Walter Chantry, "The Christian Ministry and Self Denial," BTM (November 1979): 22-23.

[180] Buess, Discipleship, 53. Buess makes a telling comparison with world leaders: 'You have seen this work in ungodly governments when they want to destroy men who are leaders. These men usually will not submit to their ungodly programs. Dictators remove natural leaders and replace them with small men who know how to rubber stamp their superiors. These are yes men.'

The high view of leadership that covering theology espouses creates many problems. The effects on Christians are no longer 'notoriously difficult to find.' Moore documents many experiences of Christians leaving the Shepherding Movement and notes that 'if the one-on-one pastoral relationship broke down, then so did the person's relationship to the church.'[181] There are many published accounts of discouraged and disillusioned Christians who have been hurt by authoritative leaders and who have had their relationship with the Church affected because of this.

There is a real danger that Christians will violate their own consciences in their willingness to submit to a church leader. Romans 14 and 1 Corinthians 8 deal with this scenario. In covering theology, a new priesthood implicitly develops. Jerram Barrs reminds us that the role of church leaders is 'not to stand between the believer and God, but rather to lead the believer to stand before God.'[182] Perhaps most seriously, it is a wrong view of God. The Bible does not teach that God's provision and protection come to the believer if they are submitted to his delegated authority found in the church leader. Taken to its extreme, a distant deist god is formed who speaks to church leaders who then mediate him to the congregation. God's supernatural activity in the life of the individual believer is lessened, and instead of placing their trust wholly in God,

---

[181] Moore, *Shepherding*, 176.

[182] Barrs, *Shepherds*, 87.

believers place their trust in their leaders and their own submission to those leaders. After 19 years in the Shepherding Movement, Ron Burks writes the following:

> *The Enemy is the one who managed to obscure the Cross for us by tricking us to put our trust in men... The kind of control over my life that I permitted, believing it was biblical, amounted to idolatry. I committed to a man what should only be committed to God, and expected to receive from a man what can only come from God. Thinking I was doing God's will, I was actually committing spiritual adultery.*[183]

No doubt there will always be temptations to extremes in every area and doctrine of the Christian faith. Just as there may be the temptation to lord it over the flock, so there may be the temptation to refuse any authority structures at all. Our supreme example must always be found in the Lord Jesus Christ. His was the model of servant leadership, the One who 'did not come to be served, but to serve,' (Matt 20:28); the One who washed the feet of His disciples (John 13:1-17) and who took on 'the very nature of a servant' (Phil 2:7). It is therefore regrettable that Jesus' own words on leadership are missing from *Under Cover*. Matthew 20 details the request of the mother of the sons of Zebedee. Wanting her sons to receive glory and power in the kingdom of God - and almost certainly assuming that the kingdom would be manifest in the here

---

[183] Burks, Damaged, 163.

and now on earth - the Lord Jesus demolishes any hierarchical form of power-hungry leadership. His response is:

> *You know that the rulers of the Gentiles lord it over them, and their great men exercise authority over them. It shall not be so among you; but whoever would be great among you must be your servant, and whoever would be first among you must be your slave; even as the Son of man came not to be served but to serve, and to give his life a ransom for many (Matt 20:25-28).*

The New Testament uses the self-sacrificing life of service that the Lord Jesus Christ embodied as a model for Christian leaders. Ron Burks writes of how the Shepherding Movement misinterpreted such a model:

> *...it was understood that leaders served by leading - by leading, they were laying down their lives for their followers... This noble tendency was codified by Charles Simpson: 'A disciple becomes a recipient of the favour and love given him, therefore he must be desirous of being a servant worthy of that favour' [New Wine, March 1974]. In the context of the Shepherding Movement, it was the leader who was loved and favoured and the follower who served. The follower was a 'recipient of the favour and love given him,' and he 'owed' service to the leader. The emphasis placed on the leader's authority, combined with a willingness on the part of the follower to be a servant, brought about a*

great reversal of Jesus' pattern of service.[184]

Burks goes on to write that 'our system - serving those in leadership - was a perversion of Christ's example.'[185] The word translated 'lord it over' in Mat 20:25 (κατακυριεύουσιν) is also found in Mark 10:42, Luke 22:25 and 1 Pet 5:3. The phrase carries no connotations of coercion, manipulation or abuse of power. It simply means 'to rule over'. The issue is not the abuse of leadership, but the hierarchical forms of leadership and systems of authority that were practised (and are still practised) in the Gentile world. Frank Viola points out that the word is:

> ***katexousiazo****... a combination of two Greek words:* ***kata****, which means 'over'; and* ***exousiazo****, which means to 'exercise authority'. Jesus also used the Greek word* ***katakuriezo*** *in this passage, which means to 'lord it over' others. What Jesus is condemning in these texts is not oppressive* ***leaders*** *as such. He's condemning the hierarchical* ***form*** *of leadership that dominates the Gentile world.*[186]

Critics of covering theology are often caricatured as anti-authority, individualistic rebels who want to live their lives their own way with no submission to any authority - including God's.

---

[184] Ibid., 94.

[185] Ibid., 98.

[186] Viola, *Reimagining*, 156.

However, as Leighton Tebay says, it is ironic that it is the proponents of covering theology themselves who are at risk of rebellion as they claim an authority that only belongs to God. They also display an almost breathtaking ignorance of church history. He writes:

> *In their attempts to patch together the disparate passages that make up their case for coverings they have to neglect centuries of orthodox biblical interpretation and the very foundations of the Reformation and Evangelicalism.*[187]

Is Bevere heretical? There are three Hebrew words that can be translated as 'covering'. The first, *sakak*, means 'to cover, or hedge in.'[188] Strong says that, in its figurative sense, the word means 'to protect...to cover, defend, hedge in, join together, set, or shut up.'[189] The second Hebrew word is *kasah* - its primary meaning is 'to cover for clothing or secrecy,'[190] - while the third word is *kaphar*. The King James Version of the Bible translates this word as 'to make atonement' and the root also means 'to cover over, pacify,

---

[187] Tebay, "Covering," n.p. Such ignorance is hardly surprising in the light of Bevere's own lack of awareness of the Shepherding Movement which was at its height 20 years prior to the publication of *Under Cover*.

[188] Robert Young, *Analytical Concordance to the Bible* (Grand Rapids: Eerdmans, 1970), 209.

[189] James Strong, *The Exhaustive Concordance of the Bible*, (New York: Blingdon Press, 1965), 82.

[190] Strong, *Concordance*, 56.

make propitiation.'[191] The chief meaning of 'covering' used by Bevere is in its meaning of 'to protect' (*sakak*). However, as Steve Coleman says, when examining the classic Shepherding/Discipleship and covering doctrine that 'we do not obey those in authority because they are right; we obey them because they are in authority, and all authority ultimately stems from God Himself'[192] this claim is not only for '*sakak* covering' but for '*kaphar* covering'. The long summary is worth quoting in full:

> *...the implication is that people could do something that is normally considered sin, i.e. something that is out of God's will. A person may know it is sin, but does not have to worry about it because he is 'covered' by a shepherd. A person will not be judged for the sin, but for his submission to the shepherd. If this is the case, then how would a sin become an act of obedience? The only answer is that this transformation occurs through the process of 'covering.' In summary...We obey our shepherd, but our action is against God's will. We are 'covered' through our submission to a shepherd. Because of our submission, the sin becomes an act of righteousness. If our sin could be transformed in this way, it could only be through **kaphar** covering. Only through **kaphar**, or atonement, could sin thus be removed, annulled and wiped*

---

[191] Francis Brown, S.R. Driver & Charles A Briggs, *A Hebrew and English Lexicon of the Old Testament: With an Appendix Containing the Biblical Aramaic* (Oxford: The Clarendon Press, 1968), 497.

[192] Prince, *Discipleship*, 18.

out. In other words, the Shepherding Movement teaches that atonement or propitiation comes through the shepherd and the authority to which we are submitted.[193]

Such a summary is implicit throughout *Under Cover*. If a believer is living the Christian life in fear of disobeying a church leader; if they believe that they will be judged by God primarily on how well they obeyed that leader; if they believe that doing what their church leader says protects them from the devil and demonic assault; if they believe that their faith and their ability to receive supernatural healing from God are in relation to their level of submission to a church leader, then it is clear that covering theology is an aberrant, wrong system of doctrine. It is a misinterpretation of Scripture and leads to idolatry, fear and 'spiritual adultery'. Leighton Tebay asks whether the requirement to come under the authority of church leaders is more like a new law or whether it is part of living by the Spirit? He writes:

The obligations of the mosaic law were onerous but at least they were consistent. A new law founded on the authoritative whims of church leaders has the potential to be far more of a burden...[194]

---

[193] Steve Coleman, Article online, 'Shepherding Covering and the MSOG'

[194] Tebay, "Covering," n.p.

The law brought slavery and death. There are many tales of spiritual abuse and shipwrecked faith that people have suffered under the auspices of 'Shepherding' and 'Discipling.' The covering theology advocated in John Bevere's *Under Cover* only adds to this detrimental effect on the Church.

BIBLIOGRAPHY

Barrs, Jerram. Shepherds & Sheep: *A Biblical View of Leading and Following.* Downers Grove: InterVarsity Press, 1983.

Bauer, Walter. *A Greek-English Lexicon of the New Testament and Other Early Christian Literature.* Chicago: University of Chicago Press, 2000.

Beardmore, Roger., ed. *Shepherding God's Flock: Essays on Leadership in the Local Church.* Harrisonburg, VA: Sprinkle, 1988.

Bevere, John. *Under Cover: The Promise of Protection Under His Authority.* Nashville: Thomas Nelson, 2001.

Brown, Francis, S.R. Driver & Charles A Briggs. *A Hebrew and English Lexicon of the Old Testament: With an Appendix Containing the Biblical Aramaic.* Oxford: The Clarendon Press, 1968.

Buckingham, Jamie. "The End of the Discipleship Era." *Ministries Today* (January/February 1990): 46, 48.

Buess, Bob. *Discipleship Pro and Con.* Texas: Buess, 1975.

Burgess, Stanley M. and Eduard M. Van Der Maas, eds. *The New International Dictionary of Pentecostal and Charismatic Movements.* Grand Rapids: Zondervan, 2002.

Burks, Ron & Vicki. *Damaged Disciples: Casualties of Authoritarian Churches and the Shepherding Movement.* Grand

Rapids: Zondervan, 1992.

Calvin, John. *Hebrews and 1 & 2 Peter.* Calvin New Testament Commentaries 12. Grand Rapids: Eerdmans, 1994.

Chantry, Walter. "The Christian Ministry and Self Denial." Banner of Truth Magazine. November 1979: 22-23.

Chrnalogar, Mary Alice. *Twisted Scriptures: Breaking Free From Churches That Abuse.* Grand Rapids: Zondervan, 1997.

Cousar, Charles B. Galatians: *A Bible Commentary for Teaching and Preaching.* Kentucky: John Knox Press, 1982.

Fitzmyer, Joseph A. *Romans.* Anchor Yale Bible Commentary 33. New York: Doubleday, 1993.

Garrett, James W. "New Testament Church Leadership in the Local Church." No pages. Cited 21 November 2011. Online: http://www.doulospress.org/pprs.php.

Green, Jay P., ed. *The Interlinear Bible: Hebrew-Greek-English.* Peabody, MA: Hendrickson, 2005.

Johnson, David and Jeff Van Vonderen. *The Subtle Power of Spiritual Abuse: Recognising & Escaping Spiritual Manipulation and False Spiritual Authority within the Church.* Minneapolis: Bethany House, 1991.

Kay, William K. *Apostolic Networks in Britain: New Ways of Being Church.* Milton Keynes: Paternoster Press, 2007.

Lambert, Steven. *Charismatic Captivation: Authoritarian Abuse and Psychological Enslavement in Neo-Pentecostal Churches.* Chapel Hill NC: Real Truth Publications, 2003.

Ligon, Bill. *Discipleship: The Jesus View. An Alternative to Extremism.* New Jersey: Logos International, 1979.

McCallum, Dennis. "Leadership and Authority in the Church: What It Is and Isn't." No pages. Cited 21 November 2011. Online: www.xenos.org/classes/leadership/leadershipandauth.html.

Moo, Douglas J. *The Epistle to the Romans.* New International Commentary on the New Testament. Grand Rapids: Eerdmans, 1996.

Moore, S. David. *The Shepherding Movement: Controversy and Charismatic Ecclesiology.* London: T & T Clark International, 2003.

Morris, Leon. *The Epistle to the Romans.* Grand Rapids: Eerdmans, 1988. Mumford, Bob. "A Most Timely Book." New Wine (May 1972): 32.

Nance, Terry. *God's Armor Bearer: Serving God's Leaders.* Shippensburg: Destiny Image Publishers, 2003.

Nee, Watchman. *Spiritual Authority.* New York: Christian Fellowship Publishers, 1972.

Prince, Derek. *Discipleship, Shepherding, Commitment.* Florida:

Derek Prince Publications, 1976.

Ramey, Tyler. "What's Wrong with John Bevere's *Under Cover*?" No pages. Cited 21 November 2011. Online: http://www.truth-enterprises.com/

Sawyer, M. James. "Under Cover: Authority, Obedience (& Abuse?)" No pages. Cited 21 November 2011. Online: http://www.reclaimingthemind.org/blog/2009/04/under cover-authority-obedience-abuse/

Strong, James. *The Exhaustive Concordance of the Bible.* New York: Blingdon Press, 1965.

Tebay, Leighton. "Covering and Authority." No pages. Cited 21 November 2011. Online:http://coveringandauthority.com/

Tsumura, David Toshio. *The First Book of Samuel.* New International Commentary on the Old Testament. Grand Rapids: Eerdmans, 2007.

Viola, Frank. *Reimagining Church: Pursuing the Dream of Organic Christianity.* Colorado Springs: David C. Cook, 2008.

Vrankovich, Mark. "Church Leadership Authority." No pages. Cited 21 November 2011. Online: http://www.cultwatch.com/ChurchLeadershipAuthority.html.

Walker, Andrew. *Restoring the Kingdom: the Radical Christianity of the House Church Movement.* Guildford: Eagle, 1998.

Young, Robert. *Analytical Concordance to the Bible.* Grand
Rapids: Eerdmans, 1970.

*N.B. Since this book was originally written in 2012, internet links
may no longer work. They have nevertheless been left in their
original form, so that the originals could be sourced where desired.*

ACKNOWLEDGEMENTS

Many thanks to Fr. Phil Ritchie for reading this book and very kindly writing the foreword. Many thanks to Daniel Emlyn-Jones for formatting, proof-reading and preparing the manuscript for publication. Many thanks to Emeritus Professor Chris Emlyn-Jones for providing the Greek fonts for the New Testament Greek examples.

And many thanks to all my family and friends who have supported me over the years.

CONTACT THE AUTHOR

The author can be contacted by email at:

AllanClarePublishing@Protonmail.com